THE FIDO-

GH00863859

A comprehensive guide to dog training & behaviour.

A balanced, intelligent approach using psychology and reward based training.

Keith Fallon
Master Trainer (Guild of Dog Trainers)
Canine Behaviourist (CFBA)

Nadine Carr
Canine Behaviourist & Trainer

EST 2013
COTSWOLD
— pet services —

Dogs are NOT humans

Accepting this simple statement is the key to

successfully training your dog.

Every creature has needs. It is the understanding of these needs, as well as the interaction with others which becomes the key to success in life.

We bring dogs into our lives and expect them to immediately understand our spoken language, but what effort do we make to learn **DOG**?

The answer for most owners is **NONE!**

Understanding your dog will help you, and your dog, to enjoy your lives together. This book will provide help and guidance as you embark upon a natural form of training -

REWARD BASED TRAINING

"To John Fisher, a visionary, whose ideas inspired me to 'Think dog'
To those dogs who have taught me so much, and remind me that there is still so much still to learn:-

Anna whom I took to Crufts at the age of 18 months as part of the Welsh Competition Obedience Team.
Bramble, my trusty companion, who reminds me that you have to work with natural instinct rather than fight against it."

Nadine Carr – co-author of the Fido Fax

Section 7— **Behavioural Issues**

Useful contact information

Vets

Trainer

Grooming Parlour

Insurance Company

Training Notes

Training Notes

Section 1

How the dog thinks and learns

<u>Success or failure</u>

What makes for an obedient dog?

Is it one that can sit?

Is it one that can lay down?

Is it one that can pick up items?

Is it one that can bark?

In essence your answers to all of these questions will be **YES**. The funny thing is that a dog can do all of this naturally, the problem is invariably **WHEN**, **WHERE** and for **HOW LONG**. This is where **WE** have the problem.

So what factors influence how successful you will be
at producing a happy and obedient dog?

The answer is simple:-
- the dog
- the owner
- the teacher (how you teach the dog)

We need to briefly examine each aspect to understand their interaction and how this affects the way you maintain your future relationship with your dog.

THE DOG

Factors

Breed - age - sex - previous history / training

BREED

Every breed has its own characteristics and understanding these can help you on the journey to success. Working strains like collies and gundogs, such as spaniels are quick learners of both good and bad habits, however with intelligence comes the potential for problems. If the dog is not stimulated it will find other things to do, and you can be assured it will not be what **YOU** want.

Some breeds, by nature, can be lazy or stubborn so expectations and methods may need to be adjusted.

AGE

A young dog is like a sponge, ready to soak up everything. You need to make sure that what they are learning is what you want them to learn. They are quick to learn, but do not rush or make lessons too long.

Older dogs can often concentrate for longer, but are usually slower to learn new skills.

SEX

Generally bitches are more biddable and easier to train.

Males, especially if they have not been neutered, can be strong minded and will try to become **TOP** dog.

THE OWNER

Factors

Age - sex - previous history / training

It is easier for a dog to train its owner than for the owner to predict what the dog will do.

People begin their training with the best of intentions, keen and with conviction, but then external factors can cause that conviction to waiver.

Simple factors like:-

- the mood we are in
- how tired we are
- how training is progressing

All too often owners lack knowledge in key areas which can adversely affect the success of the training regardless of how keen they may be.

Ask yourself:-

How well do you speak dog?

Do you know how your dog thinks?

Do you know how do dogs learn?

Knowledge, or lack thereof, of these fundamentals **WILL** influence your level of success as an owner.

THE TRAINER / TEACHER

Factors

Previous history / experience / beliefs

In the past training has focused on the attitude of the human

' Me human, you dog,

you do as I say or I will hit you'

This relies on force and aggression and can only lead to the dog resisting the force and using aggression to say NO

Then came the **'Positive reward training'**. Here the theory is that if you reward the behaviours you want but ignore those **YOU** do not want the dog is ex-pected to learn what is required of it.

The success of this method relies on the person training the dog to have a great sense of timing to be able to deliver the reward at the right moment. A second or two delay and you could be rewarding the wrong behaviour. Some behaviours are their own, regardless of what we do. For example some dogs just enjoy barking and we can ignore it as much as we like, but the dog will still get his own reward, like a 'chatty' person.

Psychology based learning is a natural way for a dog to learn.

We create the circumstances in which the dog performs the action or behaviour we want and then we reward it. When the action is predictable we are able to it a 'name' or command and reward accordingly.

The behaviour we do not want must be being rewarded in some way and we have to establish what the reward is and where it is coming from. If we can stop the reward we stop the behaviour.

In essence by understanding how a dog thinks and what motivates a dog, and by 'speaking' its language you can communicate with your dog in ways it can and will understand.

Communication is not just speaking, it is your behaviour, your mannerisms, and your own perception of yourself - after all if you see yourself as being there to serve your dog, the dog will quickly adopt the role of master.

Your success will be based upon gaining the respect of your dog.

Five Key Components of Training

When you set about teaching a dog something new there are five parts to the establishment of a behaviour.

1.   **Establishing the wanted behaviour**
2.   **Associating the signal / command with the behaviour**
3.   **Obeying the signal / command**
4.   **Proofing the behaviour**
5.   **Maintaining the behaviour**

A dog will not obey a signal / command every time, in every location, regardless if it has been thoroughly taught the possibilities . This may seem obvious, and yet so often people begin well and once the dog shows it has improved in it's behaviour in any outcome, they cut back on training.

Later they feel the dog is deliberately being naughty and not doing what you taught him.

Not so, dogs are unable to feel many of the emotions we do and certainly not revenge.

We first lure the dog into doing what we want with a treat and reward the behaviour to build an association between a sound, his reaction and pleasure.

For example the recall, '**COME**' or a whistle mean nothing to Fido. He must be taught that the sound '**Come**' or the whistle happens when he is sat in front of you and to ensure he remembers it in a pleasurable way we give him a treat, or his food.

Done several times a day for a week or so and he has learnt being around you is great and that sound is associated with it.

Gradually as we develop the dog's association with the sound and pleasure we also develop his desire to obey.

But so far this is done in the house with little or no distractions, but soon we have to move outside and '***proof***' the behaviour and this is when many people fall short in training.

They either did not spend enough time in the proofing, removed the reward too soon, or did not set the dog up to do it right.

The result is that the behaviour has not become a habit and it will be done regardless but when something more interesting comes along the dog goes wrong.

Maintaining the behaviour is vital and should include occasional rewards.

Over use of treats can sicken a dog but no use at all will have an effect and the above mentioned benefits will be lost.

HOW A DOG THINKS & LEARNS

Factors

Breed - age - sex - previous history / training

A dog's view on life is, like ours, driven by needs such as:-

food, shelter, love / reproduction, and a sense of belonging

A dog, like a child, learns by trial and error and by observing and listening to others in its pack.

When we take a dog into our lives we become its pack; **this is not optional.** As a puppy a dog begins to explore its world and find out who is pack leader and its place in the pack hierarchy – this position is flexible.

A pack of dogs has a structure which includes:- a leader, the Alpha or top dog. Every group MUST have a leader, if you do not become the leader (or mate of the pack leader) then the dog will perceive that the role is vacant and depending on breed and sex it will look to fill the role.

What makes an ALPHA?

- The Alpha sets the rules and MUST be consistent.
- The Alpha always goes through entrances first and walks in front of the rest of the pack.
- The Alpha eats first choosing the best bits.
- The Alpha guards the pack and wards off any threats.
- The Alpha can sit or lie down anywhere and has special places where no one else can sit or lie unless invited. Allowing a dog to share your special place (the bedroom for example) is inviting a challenge to your leadership role.

BRAVE NEW WORLD

Until recently dog ownership tended to be by people who needed a dog to help them with their work, like a shepherd, gamekeeper, ratters and poachers.

'Pet' dogs tended to be the province of the rich who favoured what are now called 'toy' breeds - the master of the house would have his hunting dogs.

The poorer people would look to cats which at least earned their keep and caught their own food.

After the war as people became more affluent, there was a rise in dog ownership with many formerly working breeds being kept purely as pets.

This affluence also saw a change in lifestyles with central heating becoming commonplace resulting in doors being left open to aid the distribution of heat. Upholstered furniture and fitted carpets became the norm and viewed as status symbols and changed every few years rather than when worn out.

In this brave new world dogs were free to roam the house and find their own 'special' place, usually on a chair in a commanding position having a view of the door.

The growth of effective family planning resulted in families having children later in life and so a dog, or two (so that they are company for each other while the owners are at work), become surrogate children.

These pet dogs are then often viewed as small, fluffy humans and the phrases
'he understands everything I say' and 'she is my little baby' become commonplace.

The final phase of this change in how dogs live with us was owning a second car for mum to take the kids to school and then on to the park for the dogs to 'have a run'. Previously the dog would have joined the family in the walk to school.

All this affluence and changes in lifestyle have given dogs all the signals that they are the Alpha in its pack.

Take a few minutes to contemplate on what you have just read and how your human pack behaves and the role of the dog within it.

It is time to ask yourself the following questions to see if you are giving your dog the right messages:-

- How much of the house is out of bounds to your dog, is there anywhere it cannot go?

- When you get to doors, gates etc. Who goes through first?

- Does your dog eat any meals before you, including breakfast?

- Is your dog territorial and therefore barks a lot?

- Does your dog growl when anyone approaches, when it is eating, playing with a toy or on its bed / chair?

- Does your dog 'demand' attention (nuzzle your hand) without being invited?

- If your dog is settled comfortably, does he come quickly when called?

You may have a dog with no desires to be Top Dog, in which case you are lucky and the questions asked here will not matter too much.

If however your dog views itself as a potential Alpha then you could be 'teaching' the dog to behave 'inappropriately' without realising.

Remember your dog, however cute, cuddly & sweet is still at heart a WOLF, indeed the poodle is genetically the closest. The instincts are still there despite countless years of selective breeding so you need to think like a dog to make training easier.

In many ways a dog learns just like us, so if it does something and receives pleasure or a reward then it increases the likelihood that it will repeat the behaviour. Conversely if something unpleasant, painful or frightening happens, it is less likely to repeat the behaviour and after several repetitions the lesson is learnt.

As pack leader we can make use of this cause & effect behaviour with titbits and verbal praise to reward the dog when it does what we want.

Take care not to provide a reward to STOP bad behaviour which is already in progress.

As pack leader we can also reprimand the dog when it behaves inappropriately. This does not mean beating the dog, but rather verbal reprimand or a good growl can often put the dog in its place.

Throughout your lessons you will learn how and when to praise, reward and as well as when it is appropriate to reprimand.

One very important aspect to the dog's learning process which differs to ours is when learning something new. For example if I teach you to do something and give you a command you know that whenever and wherever you get that command you must act as instructed.

In contrast a dog learns an action and command, by repeating this in the same place each time then it learns that behaviour. Give that same command in new surroundings and the likelihood is that the dog will not know how to respond and often we, as trainers fail to understand and punish the dog for not responding as we wanted. **This is not the dog's fault it is ours as the trainer.**

Instead what we need to do is once the dog responds correctly to our command in one place we need to repeat the lesson in lots of different places. Once you start these commands in new places do it one at a time, master the exercise there before moving on.

Each time the dog will respond quicker to this 'new' lesson and after a while it will see that wherever and whenever the command is given it must respond.

To quote Ian Dunbar:

> **" If you have to keep repeating a command then your dog does not know what he should be doing"**

Timing, Praise & Treats

Rewarding the dog - treats ?

What is important in training is that the dog knows when and what he has done is **RIGHT**. In order to create the desire within him to do that action (what we want) again he must associate it with something pleasurable - for most dogs this will be food. Therefore, during training using tasty treats will build that positive association.

Later play can be introduced as the reward for doing what was required; in some dogs play can be used from the beginning as they are not overly interested in food and so the play becomes the reward.

Reward based training

This is very simple in concept:- Get your dog to do want you want, give praise and reward with treats and the dog is likely to repeat the behaviour and eventually learn how to 'behave'. However in practice it is a little more complex, but with a little forethought and planning you have the tools to do the job right.

Praise and reprimand

For a dog it is not important what you say, it is the tone you use and what associations you build that will let FIDO know he did good or got it wrong. **On no account do you need to hit him, yank the lead, tweek his ear or anything else.**

Your voice is your most powerful tool, remember not volume, his hearing is far more acute than yours; yes even when he is asleep on the chair and does not 'hear' you tell him to get off. He heard, but chose not to move, a totally different matter.

(**See section 1 – 10 Brave New World**)

When you begin to teach your dog what praise is, use a soft friendly voice, use your hands to rub him and give him treats at the same time as your '**Good Boy'**. He will soon associate the words with a good feeling and a pat, the treats will soon phase out.

Similarly a growly '**BAD DOG'** or '**NO**' will explain that he has been naughty, but make sure that he knows what he should be doing and make sure that your timing is right in both cases.

(**See Timing 1 - 14**)

Treats

Always a contentious aspect of dog training - are treats bribery?

Only if used wrongly.

Treats are used initially to lure the dog into doing something we want it to do, such as:-

- Reward the dog for doing something good
- Improve the quality of an exercise

Once the dog is doing the exercise we want we no longer use the treat as a lure. For example with the sit, once he sits to a hand signal, we do not have to have the treat in that hand, but we can reward him with a treat from the pocket or the other hand and, of course, give praise. Gradually we can phase out the treat as we develop the sit, perhaps just rewarding for a quick sit, eventually no treats – just praise.

You need to consider the quality of the treats too. It needs to be small and quick to eat, very nice to eat and smelly enough to act as a lure. Each dog is different and you need to experiment to find out what he likes. I use two grades of treat – the £100 pay out and the £1000! When teaching something new I use the best one first and once he has grasped the principle I give the £100 pay out, keeping the 'good stuff' for the next new lesson.

Finally if you have a dog who is not interested in treats, then play must be used as the reward along with verbal praise right from the beginning.

Timing

Timing is the most important part of reward based training. It is imperative that the praise / treat or reprimand (withholding of praise) come just as the dog has done what was requested or is being naughty; easy to say, not so easily done.

The less experienced trainer will take a split second longer to act and can quickly find themselves rewarding the wrong action. A useful example it to watch your pup / dog and as he starts to move say 'One, one thousand, two, one thousand' and see how far he moves in that time. That is how long you have to get your praise / reward given for it to be effective and meaningful to your dog.

So give some thought to rewarding **FIDO** and if need be, practice away from him to get yourself ready. Get this idea clear in your mind, practice beforehand. Do not be afraid to stop through your praise, as if the moment has been lost, it is better than rewarding the wrong behaviour.

The following is a true story.

A lady in a training class had a dog (let's call him Mouthy) that barked when it saw another dog, nothing nasty, just vocal.

The trainer advised distracting the dog with treats to teach a new way to view other dogs. She did not explain about timing, so the novice handler duly gave the distraction treats when a new dog entered the hall.

In no time at all despite the owner's best efforts Mouthy' s barking was worse. Why? The trainer had not explained about timing, both when and how quickly.

What the trainer should have explained is that there are a few seconds when Mouthy has seen the other dog, but not yet started barking.

That was the moment to distract, praise and give treats, so he would thus learn that silence is the way to greet others. What she was inadvertently teaching was 'Yes that is it, bark when you see other dogs and you will be rewarded'.

One last word on timing, positive reward training takes as long as it takes - dogs need time to figure out what to do. So do not start a new lesson unless you can spend the time waiting for the 'penny to drop'.

Section 2

Communicating with your dog

FIDO'S GUIDE TO SPEAKING DOG

How do we take all this information and turn it into an effective way to train our dog in other words :-

'How do we speak dog?'

Never forget dogs have excellent hearing, can sit, lay down and be quiet. What we want is for them to do these things when we say.

- Firstly keep the command words simple and sufficiently different, despite our belief dogs do not understand every word we say. They pick up on key words, tone of voice, habits, behaviour and body language.

- Be consistent with your command word for a particular behaviour. Use the dog's name to get its attention then the command word for example:-
-

`FIDO , SIT'

- When starting something new initially do it in the same place each time to give your dog the best chance of success.

- Then move the exercise remembering that the level of distractions will increase especially out of doors. After 3 weeks of doing something correctly the dog has learnt the behaviour.

- Lots of short sessions are better than one long one and do not keep on repeating it over and over again as this is inviting failure and therefore 'reprimand'
- think how you would feel. Each session should involve the exercise no more than three times, but repeat the session several times a day.

- The lessons must be brought into everyday life as soon as possible and not restricted to specific times of day. The skills are there to make the dog better behaved in all aspects of its life.

**<div align="center">Most dogs are not born bad,
they learn to be 'bad',
often by what we do or do not do.</div>**

Your dog does not have a problem with its behaviour, it is just
 being a dog and acting according to its position in its pack. You are the one with the problem with your dog's behaviour and it is for you to train the dog, in ways it can understand, to behave in the manner you want.

To sum up

- Be consistent

- Be clear in what you want

- Be sure you know what you are going to do and how you will respond depending on the actions of the dog.

- Be patient, in most cases your dog is not trying to wind you up or frustrate you, it really wants to please **Alpha**. If things are not going well, swap to something simple and that the dog can do well then leave it, try again the next day.

What did Fido say ?

Dogs inherit their ability to communicate with other dogs regardless of breed and country of origin.

They communicate instructions for cooperation on a hunt, training their young, and most importantly **TO PREVENT CONFLICT** when tempers are lost. It is far too dangerous for problems to be solved by fighting, the whole pack can suffer when key members get injured.

When Fido comes to live with humans (and any existing pets) we
become pack, his pack; the problem is that we do not think like a dog or speak like a dog or behave like a dog.

WE HAVE A PROBLEM.

Our first reaction is to talk to the **DOG** as if it was a small **HUMAN** child that has already begun to understand human speech.

Surprise, surprise, Fido does not speak human!

In nature most communication, some sources say over 90%, is non verbal. This applies to both humans and our Fido. To Fido non verbal communication is second nature, to we humans it is almost another foreign language.

Sometimes we recognise when a situation is becoming 'heated' and we use **'CALMING SIGNALS'** like saying **'Calm down'** or **'Take a chill pill'** . Unfortunately, we do not recognise the calming signals made by our dog and usually we respond wrongly, which leads to frustration and aggression on our part and nervousness and stress on the part of the dog.

This stress can be directed towards people or other dogs causing them to react aggressively because your dog has given up using the **'calming signals'** because his pack does not 'listen' or understand and respond correctly.

SIGNALS
Featuring 'Bramble' the English Springer Spaniel

Nature's Calming Signals (and Fido's)

Being social animals a dog, like a human, has a wide range of non verbal signals. Here are some of the more common and obvious from the 30 or so your dog knows and could use.

Yawning

Dogs yawn because, like us, they get tired or bored, but they also use the 'yawn' to show that they feel the situation to be threatening in their eyes.

For example, if someone they do not know is bending over them, say at the vets or grooming parlour then the 'yawn' is a warning sign.

A stranger walking straight towards your dog will require you as pack leader to take action by way of a 'greeting' or adjustment of position to defuse the potential 'attack' and not put the dog into the situation where it has to defend the pack.

Arguments within the household, pushing the dog too fast or too long in training, telling the dog off by shouting are all potentially 'aggressive' situations which could elicit a negative response from the dog.

So remember a yawn may be just that, but it may also be Fido trying to tell you that "I'm stressed, I need help, calm down and "**BACK OFF**."

Nature's Calming Signals (and Fido's)

Licking

Another common calming signal is licking , not all licking,
sometimes a dog licks its lips as we would, after all we are animals just the same.

Stress related licking is usually best seen when facing the dog, when it is often just the tip of the tongue flicks in and out quite quickly.

Again many of the threatening situations, as perceived by the dog, which trigger 'yawning' can also trigger the 'lick', it is what is happening or what has just happened which **should** give us humans the whole picture.

Do remember sometimes licking is just that, but it might also be that your dogs is trying to deal with a stressful situation and is telling you "**Back Off**", "**stop doing that, give me a break**"

Nature's Calming Signals (and Fido's)

Turning away

This is used by dogs, and humans, to make another do /human calm down and stop behaving in a threaten manner/being annoying.

It can range from just a slight movement of the head to one side to moving the whole body - what would be described as cowering.

Again this can be used in many different situations, a direct (head on) approach by a stranger, bending over to stroke, an extended training session or one that is too difficult for him to understand, or if startled.

The key is to **WATCH** your dog and also study other humans when you are out and about, it is surprising what you will see.

Play bow

We have all seen this situation, but what is being '**said**'?

We assume that is an invitation to play, and often it is. If the legs / body are moving then this is the most likely message.

If however the dog remains still, then the message is different. You will see this when your dog meets another whom it has not met before, and here the message is **'keep calm'**, I am not a threat'. The human equivalent would be 'Have you heard the one about ....'

Nature's Calming Signals (and Fido's)

Walking slowly

A dog views speed differently to us, a person moving quickly towards them is threatening, whereas someone moving slowly is calming. When training to encourage your dog to feel safer, especially when teaching a new exercise which involves leaving and returning to your dog, walk back slowly.

In the recall, does your dog come back slowly?. If so consider **YOUR** behaviour, is your voice encouraging and friendly or threatening & angry?

Study your dog when it is next coming back to you and if it moves slowly consider why, is there something threatening to him that he wants calming down / dealing with?

Freeze

When faced with a dangerous / frightening situation an animal will take one of four actions:-

FIGHT - FLIGHT - FAFF - FREEZE

When a dog stops suddenly and remains totally motionless it is saying '**If you calm down and be good we do not have a problem**' The freeze can be adopted either stood up or the dog might sit down with its back to the '**aggressor**'.

This same response can be used by us if the dog is the aggressor, by standing still and saying / doing nothing we are using a calming signal the dog **may** know.

Nature's Calming Signals (and Fido's)

Walking in a curve

Dogs view a direct face on approach as potentially threatening, and will adopt a curved route as a calming signal towards the
other dog / human. A dog forced to approach something it views as frightening or dangerous can become very stressed and even aggressive.

So when meeting new dogs or strangers allow your dog a bit of room, loosen the lead to allow the dog to make its approach on the curve and show a 'calming' signal.

If you are approaching a dog, do so on a curve not a direct line and if the dog is aggressive make the curve wider.

These are just some of the signals used by dogs to defuse stressful or frightening moments.

Study your dog and you will find that you will begin to understand his language and be able to communicate with him much better.

What he is saying when meeting a new dog, and suddenly acts like a puppy, jumping around, getting **'fizzy'** and being silly?

Is it "**wow, this is exciting let's play**" or perhaps it is "**Wow, this is scary, let's all calm down and be nice**"

DOG'S action	Your command
Walking - without pulling	
Lie down	
Come to call	
Stand	
Sit	
Cease sitting	
Handling (for grooming etc.)	

Commands

KISS - Keep Instructions Simple

Remember!
DOGS DO NOT UNDERSTAND ENGLISH / FRENCH / GERMAN etc. what they will do, with training, is connect a sound / tone with a desired action. From the dog's point of view it does not matter what your word (s) of command are for example you could use the word **'ROSEBUD'** to get the dog to **'SIT'**

Pick your commands carefully, make sure that they are easy for you to remember and clear in pronunciation for the dog, then
BE CONSISTENT.

Some general words that become very useful in training are **'GOOD'** and **'NO'**

When I start something new I use **'Good dog/girl/boy'** and
accompany this with a treat.

Then as the skill is developed I use **'Good'** but no treat to show the dog they are doing what I want & keep doing it.

Then **' Good dog'** plus a treat at the end of the exercise with lots of fuss to complete the reward.

When the dog goes wrong a firm **'NO'** in a growly voice will often stop them, then give the command of what they should do and praise.

Eventually you will only need a firm **'NO'** to show wrong behaviour and when the dog obeys praise it.

The following table shows a few of the basic actions you require your dog to do, it is for you to decide what your command will be.

Section 3

Equipment

Equipment

Throughout your dog's life there will be some basic pieces of equipment he will need, some of which may need replacing as he grows out of it, it wears out, gets broken or lost, or is no longer suitable.
I have divided up this section into essential, useful extras & may be needed.

Essential
Sleeping quarters
All dogs, regardless of age, need a bed. For a puppy a cardboard box and an old blanket are best as puppy will no doubt chew his bed along with many other things until you teach him what he can and cannot chew.
When he is no longer destructive and close to fully grown, you can replace his box & blanket with a proper dog bed. I always put the old blanket into the new bed so that the new bed smells right.

Many people use metal crates to control where puppy can, and cannot go; I found a child's playpen useful, but a utility room is also good.
Pup needs a safe place where he can still be part of the family, safe, out of the way and can be left when the family are out or at night when the family is asleep.
See (**Section 4-11 The puppy**)

Food & water
Your dog will need the appropriate food for his age, breed and level of work.
The wrong food, regardless of how good the packaging looks, can cause lots of problems. See (**Section 7-3 Feed**)
He will need both food & water bowls, with clean fresh water always available.

Collar & lead

When he is a puppy he will need a soft, puppy collar and lead for him to get used to and that can be adjusted as he grows.
 When he finally stops growing a broad flat collar is appropriate with a lead of suitable weight & length. Fitted to the collar needs to be an identity disc with **your** surname, address & phone number

Health matters

- **Grooming tools -** Eventually you will need a small range of grooming tools suitable for his breed, but to begin with a grooming mitten is excellent to develop a love of being groomed. A few old towels will prove useful for drying him off when wet.
- **A Vet** – for his regular injections and any health problems
- **Poo bags –** when out walking with your dog you should always carry a supply of poo bags so that you can clean up after him if necessary.

Toys

Toys and play are an important role in your relationship with your dog, especially puppies, and for his well being generally. Your dog does not need lots of toys, but rather two or three well chosen ones. Activity toys, like **KONGS**, which will keep him occupied when left alone are especially good. They have the facility whereby you can put food
 inside which he then has to figure out how to get it out; this engages his brain while keeping him busy and makes the meal last longer. Teething / chewing toys are also an excellent way to channel his natural desire, and need, to chew.
(See 5 -12 Household Etiquette on Chewing.)

You will also need **YOUR TOY**. It does not matter what you choose as 'your' toy providing that you keep it as yours and when playing with your dog, always retain it and put it away and out of reach. I recommend something soft, not too big or heavy so that it can go on walks with you tucked into a pocket.

There are a host of producers of equipment for dogs, some are good whilst others are very expensive for what you get.

Remember the dog does not care how much you spent on an item, the key for the dog is

'Does it work?'

Some good options:

- **Antler Chews**. Come in different sizes and are natural and hardwearing
- New types of superb tough chew such as the **Goughnut**
- Raw Carrots—yes raw carrots! Might make a mess but cheap and natural
- Natural rope toys
- Clean, raw beef bone (not marrow). Your butcher will often be happy to supply these cut to size
- Dried fish skin treats. Bit smelly but natural and full of healthy oils
- **Kongs**. Stuff with sticky foods like peanut butter or cream cheese

Avoid if possible:

- Rawhide chews—can sometimes be preserved with chemicals
- Cooked bones—can be from dubious sources and cause upset stomachs
- Highly coloured, flavoured chews with animal derivatives
- Filled bones. *Take the filling out and put in your own filling, such as peanut butter.

Training Equipment

Once you are ready to start training you will need other pieces of equipment and again I have grouped them. Basics – the must haves, useful extras – things which will help your training, further useful extras – other very good pieces, specialist – for obedience or gundog work.

Basics

- A properly fitting broad flat collar
- Lead of appropriate length and weight for your dog
- Treats – two grades see (**Section 1-14 Treats**)
- Your Toy – see above
- Poo bags

Useful Extras

- Multi pocketed waistcoat to carry treats, toys etc. When out walking / training
- Bag to bring equipment to training classes
- A retrieving toy
- Plastic gundog whistle – This is a vital tool in recalling your dog and when used properly after the correct training aids the recall. The whistle provides:-
  ⇒ A consistent command whoever uses it and it does not reflect your mood
  ⇒ A sound that carries clearly over a greater distance than a voice
  ⇒ A command that cannot be influenced by other people when you are training or exercising your dog

  ⇒ It is wise to buy **TWO Acme Gundog** whistles with the same frequencies of either 210 or 211.5 plus a lanyard for each. In this way should you lose one you have a spare.

There are other styles of whistle - metal, silent or stag horn - but in my opinion none perform as well as the **Acme**

Specialist Extras

If you decide to take your training further, whether for fun or more seriously, there will be other pieces of equipment needed, but your
trainer will be able to explain what you need, when and where to get it.

'Happy Chappy' collar / lead is the perfect way to improve control of an over excitable dog, stop pulling and enable positive reward training to take place. The soft rope does not stretch or chaff your hands. Fitting is easy both to put on and remove and it can be used left or right handed.
The **Happy Chappy** is a gentle, pain free way to help you train your dog, so much so that it can be used on a puppy thus preventing pulling before it even begins. Available from myself or Cotswold Pet Services.

Walk your dog with Love Front Leading Stop Pull Harness.

Like many animals, humans included, dogs pull away when they are pulled on.

The harder we pull, the harder they pull; it's called oppositional pulling. With this dog harness, pulling slows things down and gives us more control, naturally.

They are lightweight and easy to fit.

Training Line /Long lead/Check cord

Available in different lengths a long lead or line can be a useful tool for teaching recall or retrieving. Look for a strong but soft line as many long lines are made from a flat hard plastic that can cause nasty friction burns.

Opt for one with a handle on the end and always tie a few knots in your line so that you have something to grab!

Clickers Popular with some training methods. This book concentrates more on other methods of rewarding such as praise along with edible rewards,toys and the forerunner of the clicker, the whistle.

Items to Play Fetch or Find

Tennis balls, rope toys, canvas gundog dummies, fur balls and dummies.

Gundog dummies are particularly good for scenting and hunting work as they are filled with sand and sawdust and absorb all kinds of smells as they are used. They usually float so also good for water retrieval.
Some dogs prefer a ball initially but with a little perseverance will learn to retrieve many different items.

Section 4

Your Dog

Responsible Dog Ownership

Whether you want it or not, once you take a puppy, or any dog, into your family home you become his pack in his den. You become personally responsible for his behaviour and must ensure that he does not inconvenience, disturb or impact on others.

You are responsible to ensure your dog is:-
- Properly fed and watered using his own bowl
- Exercised as appropriate to his breed and age
- Given company and affection
- Given a suitable place to sleep
- Shown his position in the 'pack'
- Given regular veterinary check ups, medication for worming & fleas
- Regularly groomed and checked over
- Not allowed to become a nuisance to others by running free (out of control), barking or chasing livestock
- Never let out alone
- Never allowed to foul in inappropriate places; always clean up after him.
- Taken care of when you go on holiday
- Neutered or spayed if appropriate
- Always wearing a collar with a disc giving your surname, house name or number, post code, phone number.
- Micro chipped
- Properly socialised with other dogs, people and children
- Taught how to travel safely in a car

A well trained dog is a joy to see and a responsible owner improves the views of **'non doggy'** people.
 If owners are not prepared to do what is required of a responsible owner, including cleaning up, then they fuel bad feelings in others against dogs in general.

Dog breed characteristics & behaviour

Many of the '**problem'** behaviours of our dogs stem from their basic genetic make up - a collie cannot help but herd. By having a better and deeper understanding of a dog's type we are better placed to develop and shape behaviour we want.

By nature dogs will also show traits which we would describe as being:-

Dominant / Submissive

&

Passive / Aggressive

The grid opposite shows how the breed types can be used to choose your ideal companion.

Knowing your dog's breed characteristics you are able to establish a better relationship with your dog. For example if your puppy is one of the '**Northern Breeds'** your puppy will be a natural leader, but not aggressive.

Compared with the '**Protecting'** dogs where the dominance trait combines with aggression to create breeds which require very careful and positive training.

The following are some general behavioural attributes of different breed types. These are not meant to be rules of behaviour. All dogs are individuals and have their own personality.

This information may be useful when choosing a dog, or understanding its behaviour.

Dominant

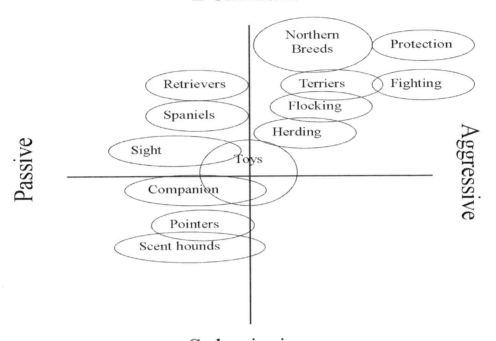

Submissive

PROTECTION DOGS

Most protection dogs were bred originally as herding dogs or flock guards. We now use them for a variety of purposes, including police work, guarding homes or property, or for specific leisure activities or sports, such a Schutzhund work.

BREEDS INCLUDE: Akita, Rottweiler, Doberman pinscher, Bull Mastiff and Mastiff, Great Dane, Boxer and Giant Schnauzer.

German Shepherd is included in this group as well as the herding group the Rhodesian Ridgeback is used as a combination guard, protection and hunting dog.

TYPICAL BEHAVIOURAL PROFILE: Confident, dominant, extremely trainable, ability to work well with humans

TYPICAL PROBLEMS: Dominant aggression, separation anxiety, possessiveness

FLOCKING DOGS & MOUNTAIN DOGS

Flock guards were bred to protect their herds of sheep or cattle from marauding predators. Many of them were bred to be white, so they would blend into the flocks. They tend to be quite protective of their families and fear very little.

The most well known in this country are the Great Pyrenees, Komondor, and Kuvasz. Closely related to the flock guards are the Mountain Dogs - St. Bernard, Newfoundland and Bernese Mountain Dogs. Also quite heavy-boned, with large, domed heads, these animals tend to be sweet-tempered, if stubborn.

TYPICAL BEHAVIOURAL PROFILE: Confident, dominant, protective, independent, tolerant, ability to work well with humans.

TYPICAL PROBLEMS: Dominant aggression, wanderlust, possessiveness.

HERDING BREEDS...

It's thought by some that herding dogs retain more "wolf" behaviours than any other type of dog except the Northern Breeds. This is because they stalk and chase (herd) on a regular basis. Herding breeds are used to herd sheep and cattle. They are often flock protectors as well. They are usually medium sized, agile, sensitive, and quick to use their teeth to move their flock.

BREEDS INCLUDE: Border Collie, Collie, Old English Sheepdog,
German Shepherd, Belgian Shepherd (3 varieties), Australian Shepherd, Heeler or Cattle dog, Kelpie, Corgi and Shetland Sheepdog, Puli, Bearded Collie and Bouvier.

TYPICAL BEHAVIOURAL PROFILE: Anxious, demanding, dominant, protective, sensitive, loyal, great obedience dogs, ability to work well with humans

TYPICAL PROBLEMS: Fear-based aggression, separation anxiety, destructive, noisy

RETRIEVERS...

Retrievers retrieve - whether in water, on land or in the air. Most retrievers are "party animals," good natured, outgoing and very energetic. People have bred specifically for particular aspects of the wolf's prey drive - the chase, and bringing the prey back to the den. In addition, these dogs need to be submissive enough to give their possessions to their owners.

BREEDS INCLUDE: Flat Coated Retriever, Golden Retriever, Curly Coated Retriever, Chesapeake Bay Retriever. Chesapeake Bay Retrievers are not usually as friendly and outgoing as the rest of the retrievers, and in fact, can be quite aggressive, since they were also used to guard property.

TYPICAL BEHAVIOURAL PROFILE: Energetic, dominant, happy, mouthy, ball or Frisbee oriented, vocal, great obedience dogs, ability to work well with humans

TYPICAL PROBLEMS: Destructive, noisy, mouthy during puppy stage, overwhelmingly energetic, separation anxiety, occasionally escape orientation or wanderlust, possessive.

SPANIELS...

The word Spaniel derives from the word "Spain." And indeed some of the group did come from that country. Spaniels are hunting dogs, bred to flush or "spring" game from bushes. They are conveniently sized for pets, and are quite popular because of that. Dogs bred for pets only generally have lots of hair - or feathering - on their ears and legs.

BREEDS INCLUDE: American Water, Clumber, Cocker, English Cocker, English Springer, English Toy, Field, Irish Water, Japanese Chin,
Sussex, Tibetan and Welsh

TYPICAL BEHAVIOUR PROFILE: Cheerful, fun-loving, energetic, "birdy," love to fetch

TYPICAL PROBLEMS: Possession, unruliness, destructiveness, mouthy. A behavioural problem known as "rage syndrome" (thought to be a form of dominant aggression or possibly conflict behaviour) is prevalent in some strains of Cockers and Springers. The behaviour is characterized by attacking and biting, with no apparent provocation.

COMPANION DOGS...

Companion dogs are essentially a mixed canine bag, ranging from the Dalmatian to the Lhasa Apso.

They don't quite fit in anywhere else. The poodle was originally a water hunting dog, the English Bulldog a sporting dog (if you call Bull baiting a sport), the Keeshond and Schipperke were barge companions, the Tibetan Terrier and Lhasa Apso guard dogs with some herding thrown in, and Boston Terrier a companion. Their temperaments are just as varied as their looks.

TYPICAL BEHAVIOURAL PROFILE: Varies from breed to breed

TYPICAL PROBLEMS: Dalmatians can be dog and people aggressive, and need vast amounts of exercise. The Schipperke is very dominant, often dominant aggressive, the Boston Terrier is feisty and independent, and the Poodle often has separation anxiety and vocal problems.

POINTERS AND SETTERS...

Pointers are highly energetic with normally happy temperaments and tolerant dispositions. The Dalmatian was originally a pointing variety, but retains little of the temperament except for the energy. Setters are also hunting dogs, often with a more sensitive or nervous disposition. The Irish Setter lost a lot of behavioural ground when it was over bred several years ago.

BREEDS INCLUDE: German Shorthair, Wirehaired and English Pointers, the Irish, English, and Gordon Setters.

TYPICAL BEHAVIOURAL PROFILE: Both types are energetic, often nervous, though most have sweet temperaments. Good with children, though not in the obedience ring.

TYPICAL PROBLEMS: Running away, disobedience, destructiveness

FIGHTING DOGS...

While the tendency to fight has been bred out of many of these dogs, it remains in others — either accidentally or purposefully. Much of their aggression comes from their prey-drive, so it is not driven by emotion. Thus, with tails wagging, fighting dogs appear to enjoy the fight. Most are very stubborn and independent. They are usually extremely bonded and affectionate with their owners, and the sound ones make great dogs for children.

BREEDS INCLUDE: Sharpei, Pit Bull Terrier, Bull Terrier, Staffordshire and Staffordshire Bull Terrier, and Akita.

TYPICAL BEHAVIOURAL PROFILE: Lively, affectionate, bonded, predatory, very focused

TYPICAL PROBLEMS: Untrustworthy with other dogs or other animals, occasionally aggressive towards humans

SCENT HOUNDS...

Scent Hounds are master smellers, in a species with an absolutely amazing ability to smell. Most Scent hounds have long ears - in Bloodhounds and Bassets, so long that the ears sometimes scrape the ground and stir up even more scents.

BREEDS INCLUDE: Beagles, basset, Otter, Coon.

TYPICAL BEHAVIOURAL PROFILE: Sweet tempered and tolerant,
excellent for families. Rarely bite.

TYPICAL PROBLEMS: Wanderlust, occasional dominance aggression, indifference to training.

SIGHT HOUNDS...

Sight hound are typically long and lean, sometimes virtually disappearing when looked down upon from above. They have keen vision, and can run miles without tiring. Most were or are used to course prey — including everything from rabbits to deer to wolves.
BREEDS INCLUDE: Afghan, Saluki, Ibizan, Pharaoh, Greyhound, whippet, Italian Greyhound

TYPICAL BEHAVIOURAL PROFILE: Reserved, sometimes shy, aloof, gentle, quiet when they're not running after something.

TYPICAL PROBLEMS: Predatory to small animals, many are not interested in obedience work, so have earned the reputation of being stubborn and stupid, which they are not.

NORTHERN BREEDS...

These dogs are beautiful, and often look like wolves (they are also used often in breeding Wolf Hybrids). A working Malamute can pull up to a ton for a short distance, while Huskies specialize in long treks. Samoyeds are all round sled dogs. American Eskimos are bred down sled dogs (as are Pomeranians). Thick double coat sheds dirt.

BREEDS INCLUDE: Alaskan Malamute, Siberian Husky, Samoyeds, American Eskimo, Norwegian Elkhound, Finnish Spitz, American Husky, Pomeranian (Akita and Chow Chow also could fall into this group)

TYPICAL BEHAVIOURAL PROFILE: Many are very independent, and have a tendency to roam if not adequately fenced. Predatory. Often quite tolerant of pain (like that delivered by a small child).

TYPICAL PROBLEMS: Wandering, killing small animals, difficult to obedience train, dominant, possessive and aggressive.

TERRIERS...
Small to medium sized dogs (one large - the Airedale), bred to chase after and kill vermin or to be the participants in dog fighting or bull baiting. Very hardy, as a rule, many with harsh, wiry coats that need little conditioning. Virtually all hail from various parts of the British Islands.
BREEDS INCLUDE: Airedale, Australian, Bedlington, Border, Boston, Bull, Cairn, Dandie Dinmont, Irish, Kerry Blue, Lakeland,
Manchester, Norfolk, Norwich, Scottish, Sealyham, Silky, Skye, Smooth Fox, Soft-Coated Wheaten, Tibetan, Toy, Fox, Toy Manchester, Welsh, West Highland White, Wire Fox, Yorkshire...and Jack Russell.
I do include Miniature Schnauzers and Dachshunds in this group, because they share the disposition.

TYPICAL BEHAVIOURAL PROFILE: Scrappy, energetic, independent, often predatory, hardy and fun describes most terriers. They can be quite dominant, and are often poor pets for kids because of their low bite inhibition. The short legged variety tend to get on better with other dogs than the longer legged types, though this is a very broad generalization.

TYPICAL PROBLEMS: Snappy, independent, dog-aggressive, dominant-aggressive, the smaller ones have trouble with house training.

TOYS...
Most of these little guys take on the breed characteristics of their larger cousins, with a few twists.

Because they're so tiny, they can often be quite snappy, no matter what breed they were bred down from, and they develop their own specific behaviour problems — especially a dislike of being put on the ground!

BREEDS INCLUDE: Affenpinscher, Brussels Griffon, Chihuahua, English Toy Spaniel, Italian Greyhound, Japanese Chin, Maltese, Toy Manchester Terrier, Miniature Pinscher, Papillion, Pekinese, Pomeranian, Toy Poodle, Pug, Shih Tzu, Silky and Yorkshire Terriers.

TYPICAL BEHAVIOURAL PROFILE: Type specific, except that they tend to be vocal.

TYPICAL PROBLEMS: Snappy, vocal, shy, separation anxiety, dominant and aggressive.

The Puppy

The Puppy

Whether you want it or not, once you take a puppy, or any dog, into your family home you become his pack in his den.

Within the first 10 / 14 days he has sorted out his priorities:-
- *Who feeds him , where and when*
- *Who is good for a cuddle*
- *Who is fun to play with*
- *Who is boss or Alpha.*

Remember, however cute and cuddly he is right now, he is still a wolf at heart. He will get bigger and grow up then what was cute now will probably not be as endearing when he is much larger, especially if he is a breed of large dogs.

Remember these few vital facts:-
- *He is not a furry four legged human sub-species*
- *He is a dog (wolf) - one you love dearly - but still a wolf*
- *He is learning from the moment he comes into your lives, make sure that he learns the right things from the beginning.*
- *He must have rules and they must be consistent ALL the time and with ALL the family.*
- *As a puppy he is like a sponge, ready to soak up information, so you do not need to wait until he is older to start training.*
- *Make learning a game and fun for everyone.*
- *Keep lessons short, especially while he is a puppy*
- *There are three key stages of development to create a good social dog - make the most of each stage.*

To illustrate how important early training is, here are the 3 developmental stages you need to understand:-

Stage 1 - up to 12 weeks of age - Socialising with people

This is very important, the puppy needs to meet as many people as possible and discover that people are nice. This needs to include men, women and children of all ages. Ideally, by the time he is 3 months old he should have met approximately 100 people (no need to keep count), this should be a gentle interaction.

Stage 2 - by 18 weeks - Learning bite inhibition

This is the next most important lesson, if you have done a good job with socialising, then there should not be any problems here, but there are always accidents, tails & paws get trodden on, children fall on dogs etc. A startled dog will react naturally with a bite. If taught bite inhibition, then the likelihood of damage is reduced.
(**Section 5-9 Bite Inhibition**)

Stage 3 - by 20 weeks - Limiting adolescent problems

As soon as your puppy has completed its injections and is safe to go out into the world and meet other dogs the clock is ticking.

Your puppy needs to continue meeting lots of nice people and further his belief that people are nice. In addition and equally important is for pup to meet lots of well mannered dogs and discover that, on the whole, most dogs are nice.

This is where well run puppy classes can help, puppies need careful introduction to others and learn how to meet, mix and eventually play nicely together. This does not mean letting a load of different pups loose in a room to have a free for all. The class bullies will pick on the wimps and neither will benefit from the experience.

Now in preparation for the rest of the dog's life, it is time to take your Fido along to lessons in training, and most importantly.....

Enjoy your dog!

Regular walks to lots of different places will again help the puppy to develop into a well rounded dog, able to cope with all of life's challenges.
 One word of caution ensure you handle these new experiences properly, that is as a **DOG** would - if we respond as a human we can inadvertently be teaching our dog the wrong things when they meet strangers, dogs and other scary things see (**Section 5 Etiquette**)

From the minute your pup arrives in your home you need to start showing him how to behave properly both inside and outside and to have decided on the House Rules.

You will have doubtless waited sometime form this bundle of joy, but remember it will not be all plain sailing, there will be times when you will question your decision, but do not be afraid to seek help and remember he will not be a pup forever.

As your pup goes out into the world take care not to over do the stimulation, he may be a sponge eager to soak up information, but even sponges can get overloaded. Some breeds seem to have limitless energy and owners often feel lots of exercise will tire them out and make for a quiet time in the home.

Young animals need their rest, need time for growth and to strengthen muscle, too much exercise can be bad for them.
So follow the rule of **5 minutes** exercise, done **twice** daily, for **every month of age** until fully grown i.e. 15 minutes twice a day at 3 months, 20 minutes twice a day at 4 months.

However exercising the brain can be just as tiring for a puppy but without the physical risks, so lots of games involving them will help.

So your fluffy, happy puppy has been well socialised, taken to training classes where, with your hard work he has learned all his lessons well and become a model student.
Then one day you ask him to do a simple task like sit and he does not, he becomes disobedient and disrespectful. He starts getting up on the furniture and refuses to give up **HIS** toy. You have just had your first encounter with the adolescent dog.

The Adolescent Dog

What has happened is that your little ball of fluff has just become a teenager!!!

Like humans, dogs are influenced by hormones and these affect
behaviour and the impact will vary from dog to dog. A well behaved child / dog can
become a 'yob' thinking that they know everything and do not listen to anyone
because they know what is best. Does this sound familiar?

Do not despair, if you did your homework beforehand then the good manners will
return. It is time to re-read your **Fido-Fax** and check out **YOUR** alpha status
and make sure that you are still in charge. Return to basics using high class treats
and be patient all will come right.

A quick refresher course of lessons will help provide support through this period of
change. With your help and guidance your dog will grow out of the 'problem' and be
nice again.

It would also be appropriate to checkout the feed and make sure that type and
volume are still correct.
See the section on **Feeding** which might also prove beneficial for calming your
adolescent dog.

Re-homing a dog

When we decide to take on an adolescent or adult dog we do not have the opportunity to see and assess the mother and other pups in the litter. Nor can we ensure that all the socialising, handling and training has been done to produce a well adjusted and happy dog.

We may be lucky enough to know / be told some of the dog's background, but most likely we will know nothing. Often a dog is re-homed because the previous owner could not cope with the dog's behaviour, size or bad habits. Whatever the dog's past, he is having a fresh start with you.

Knowledge of the dog's past is not a prediction of future behaviour, but it a useful beginning.

Here are some points for your to consider for when the dog comes into your home.

1. Start as you mean to go on - your new dog will take the first 10 / 14 days to evaluate his new pack / family. Finding out who is the '**pack**' leader and the relative positions of the other pack members. Make sure that he learns that he is **NOT** top dog. Tips can be found in **Section 1 - How the dog thinks and learns.**

2. What has passed is past. Do not try to compensate for the past. Do not feel sorry for him and his **possible** dreadful life, especially if you do not know the history IN FULL, feeling '**sorry**' leads to '**little**' indulgences to be "kind to the poor thing", the result will be that you will wake up and find you now have a problem
    - **HIM**.

3. Plan a suitable training programme - assess what he can and cannot do and shape his behaviour to fit in with his new family environment. Love him, do not spoil him. Look on him as a puppy with some knowledge and train him appropriately.

Do not expect him to learn as quickly as a puppy might, but with patience and time you can achieve good results. The system of training outlined in this folder is suitable for dogs of any age.

However, if there are sudden changes in the dog's behaviour seek a reputable behaviourist or trainer for help. It may be the past coming out or it could also be something new.

Section 5

Household Etiquette

Household etiquette

In this section there is help and guidance for the more common
problems which can arise as your pup learns to live in your human pack.

You, as **LEADER (ALPHA),** have the right to set the house/den rules and the sooner
you begin the better.

I have divided the '**rules**' into those which will be relevant to all

puppies and those which **MAY** be relevant to your puppy. Remember a problem
does not go away if you ignore it and puppies will only grow out of a problem if
shown the right way by you.

You are responsible for his welfare, general behaviour and what he does.

Handling, examination & grooming

The following comments and exercises apply equally to a puppy or any new dog into your family environment.

It is vital that a dog be able to be handled and examined by a wide range of humans, from friends and family to vets and pet professionals.
For this to be without incident the dog must be in a relaxed state of mind.

Handling should be a relaxing experience for all concerned, but to the dog this does not come naturally; some breeds find this easier than others. Stress when being handled can lead to lots of problems and suffering when trips are made to the vets or grooming parlour.

Problems can be avoided if handling is introduced early in a pup's life it makes grooming, the application of medicine, routine checks of eyes, ears paws and examination of the coat much easier.

Handling

Once your dog / puppy has had 24 hours to settle into your household try handing him to see his reaction. Some dogs immediately love being handled, but others tense up, go squirmy while they are uncomfortable and then go completely fizzy making it impossible to do anything.

Take the time with the reluctant ones to develop their love of being handled and later examined. Pick your time right, choose a point when pup has been awake for a while and had a good play and had his bathroom break.
He is going to be getting tired and ready to sleep. Get yourself comfy on a chair or the floor and encourage pup to come to you.

Make soothing noises and gently smooth from top of head and down the back, be observant, most dogs have a special place that they enjoy being rubbed or smoothed, often behind the ears or on the neck.

As you see the pup's eyes getting heavy you are on the right track, keep going and when he lays down carry on rubbing your hands gently over his body. Do not expect to much too soon, but done daily and several times a day you will soon have a pup enjoying your hands on him.

Gradually you can introduce this exercise earlier, before he is really tired, you can also introduce rolling him over on his back to rub his tummy and gently handle his paws and tail. When he is happy to have this done then start bringing in a hug with him sitting at first but later on his back. This gentle hug can also be used as a restraint for medical treatment while the dog remains happy and relaxed.

When pup really enjoys this handling with you at any time of day start introducing family members and later friends to do the same. Now it is time to introduce the examination.

Examination
As part of the daily grooming after exercise you need to check the dog's eyes to make sure no seeds have got into them, the ears for similar objects, paws for thorns, burrs and clots of muddy hair.

Teeth also need checking regularly to make sure there is no build up of tartar and in some cases daily cleaning may be needed.
The use of **antler chews** or proprietary teeth cleaning 'teeth cleaning **toys**' is recommended rather than rawhide '**sticks**' which are designed to be eaten because the latter becomes food and the additional food intake can affect a dog's behaviour.

As soon as the pup is happy to let you handle him all over introduce the touching of all these areas, use a word command for the whole process like '**lets check you over'** and for each area it can be simply '**let's check paws'** etc.
 It is not important what words you use only that you are consistent and use them at the vets as well.
This gives the dog a warning of what is expected and always praise him as you go for good behaviour.

These early examinations are there to prepare him for when he goes out into the big world and these is will be needed.

To progress from handling into grooming should be an easy step, but do not assume the pup will be happy with hard brushes and combs as compared with soft hands.

A good intermediate step is to use a grooming mitt as these have a rubber tooth **'brush'** on one side and a 'polishing cloth' on the other. As with handling introduce the mitt when the puppy is ready to settle down and rest.

Start with the smooth side and when he is happy with that swap to the rubber brush side. Use gentle strokes as, at this stage, the idea is education and not grooming.

Once he accepts, and it may not take long, you can start introducing other brushes which will be used when he grows up. Keep it gentle as this is only education, when pup is happy with these tools you can move on and introduce proper grooming sessions.

Grooming
After exercise you can bring in his grooming session, make sure that you have to hand a few treats, his grooming tools and a regular location as this will speed the development of the earlier exercises into stress free grooming that you both will enjoy.

Always remember never groom when wet, be careful over tangles in long coated dogs, cutting them out rather than trying to pull them out; **THINK HOW YOU WOULD FEEL**.

Begin grooming by placing a treat in sight of, but just out of reach of your dog. Use appropriate grooming tools for your dog and once the sit has been taught, (**Section 6 - 4**) encourage your dog to sit while grooming face, ears, neck and chest.

Give rewards frequently for good behaviour then as your dog sits / stands quietly for grooming the treats can be reduced to one at the end of the session.

Once your dog has learnt to **stand** on command (**Section 6 -14**) encourage him into a standing position for grooming his body, hind quarters and tail. Follow this up by an inspection of eyes, ears, teeth and paws, then praise and reward. Remember grooming should be done every day and the time spent early in educating him on how to behave will pay great dividends for the rest of his life and help strengthen the bond between you.

Going to the vet

The sooner your puppy learns that the vet's is a great place, the better for all concerned and it is an easy lesson.

Consider, if your puppy only goes to the vets a few times and on each occasion he gets an injection, it will not take long for him to decide :-

'I do not like going to the vets'.

He is therefore tense and misbehaves which makes treatment difficult and his worst thoughts are confirmed.
You also react to this prospect by becoming tense, which the dog picks up on and becomes tense and a self fulfilling prophecy is created. The rest of his life, and yours, will be a battle whenever he has to go to the vets.

To resolve this problem, when he is young take him in the car to the vet's just for a visit.
Arrange a convenient time with the practice nurse, take treats and then when it is his turn, place him on the table, if he is calm and happy praise him and give him a treat. Once waiting in the waiting room and going on the table can be done calmly and happily, get one of the nurses to fuss him and give him a treat.

Once this can be done happily, let he examine him whilst giving praise and treats. Repeat until the second injection is done plus a few visits after.
By then you will have a dog happy to go to the vets, calm and easy to handle, not to mention a very happy vet.

This same method can be used for the grooming parlour if you intend to have then trim, groom or bath your dog. Again start before it is needed, make it rewarding and fun, so when it is needed the dog is happy to go there.

DO NOT BE PROTECTIVE

Fido Fact – Dogs guard what is theirs –
philosophy **'Never a borrower or lender be'**
In the wild dogs do not lend their possessions, they show their status by what they eat or the bones they can chew on. I will give up something to the **Alpha** dog, but not to a dog of lower status in the pack.
In many cases people inadvertently teach their dog that it is OK to protect their food, toys, bed etc., when in fact what the dog should be taught is that he has no right, or need, to protect their things.

Often the pup is given his food and left to enjoy it in peace as everyone leaves the room.
Children are taught **'Do not disturb the dog whilst he is eating'**. This, in many ways an obvious and sensible piece of advice, however accidents will happen, and emergencies occur. The day will come when he will get disturbed and then how will he react?

If a child trips and lands on or near him while he is eating, will he feel **'Oh dear, no problem' or react aggressively**? Similarly if, for some reason, you have to remove his feed bowl while he is still eating will he say **'Of course, no problem'** or react aggressively? Decide which behaviour is preferable.
If, from the day our puppy or re-homed dog arrives you hand feed part of his meal each time and then place the rest in his bowl on the floor you are showing that you, as **Alpha**, are in control of the allocation of food.
Gradually you can skip the hand feeding the odd meal, then, do it once a day and within a week, just once a week.

Similarly when his food goes down stay in the room with him, walk around him, walk in and out of the room, stroke him. Interrupt his feeding and move his bowl to a different place in the kitchen.

Generally make sure he understands that because you are Alpha, assuming that you are also applying all of the Alpha rules (**see section 1-10 – Brave new world**), that he does not need to nor is allowed to 'protect' his food.
In this way if a child trips and lands by him/ on him when he is feeding he will not react badly.

Similarly, from the beginning encourage him to give up his toy or chew for a treat and praise. It can be given back after, but he will not then see the act of taking his toy or chew as a treat.

Bite Inhibition

It is vital that, from a very young age, a puppy learns to control his bite. Initially although the teeth are really sharp they do little damage because the jaw muscle is not yet strong enough to cause damage.

The well socialised dog is less likely to feel the need to bite as he will have learnt that people and other dogs are friendly and nice to know.

However there are those occasions when he may be startled and react out of instinct, for example when a tail or paw is stepped on or a child trips and falls on the dog. If bite inhibition has been taught then the dog is less likely to let teeth touch skin and if they do then there will be little or no damage.

This is one of the most important lessons you can teach your puppy, so read this lesson through and make it a top priority, especially if your pup's breed is more prone to being 'mouthy', i.e. Terriers and guarding breeds like the German Shepherd dog and Rottweiler.

Bite Inhibition — Lesson

DO NOT reprimand your puppy or physically punish him, but he must know that he has hurt you.

As of now you have the most sensitive skin in the world when you play with him and if his teeth touch you pretend it was a most painful bite. Make a good ' **OUCH**' or similar sound and hold the part he touched and pretend to 'lick your wounds', then call the pup over and request a sit or lay down to say sorry and make up.

Now go back to playing, if his teeth touch your skin again, then repeat the same routine. If he still does not learn then when his teeth touch your skin call him a '**BULLY**' and turn your back and walk away. Give him a few minutes to think about what happened to drive you away, then return and make up.

Gradually bring your response in for lighter and lighter touches of his teeth to your skin, until he reaches the conclusion that:-

these people seem to be very sensitive and I must be very gentle and not touch their skin - success.

Then if he gets carried away in play and touches your skin with his teeth, simply repeat the lesson again.

Toilet Training

It is time to 'potty train' your dog, not with an actual child's potty, but to toilet outside rather than on your best carpet. This is often seen as a big problem with many owners due in the main to bad advice on how to punish when pup gets it wrong. It is very important to remember that he has not been bad and should not, in any way be punished, if anyone is to blame it is you.

Toilet training is not difficult, it is simply a matter of being:-
- **OBSERVANT** of when and where your pup goes to toilet
- **CONSISTENT** in taking him outside frequently
- **PATIENT** while he 'performs', after all he has to find the 'right' place
- **PRAISE & REWARD** when he gets it right, ignore when things go wrong

There are some key times when a pup is most likely to need to relieve himself, so make a habit of encouraging him outside:-
- When he wakes up or starts moving about after resting
- When he gets excited, i.e. Upon the arrival of visitors
- After he eats or drinks
- After exercise or play
- If he sniffs the ground and / or circles
- Initially every half hour / later if he goes towards the door.

Yes, you will be going in and out a lot at first, so have a coat and treats by the door. This will not last forever and it will be worthwhile in the long run.

It is also very helpful to have a place where pup will be confined at night - a wash-clean floor makes cleaning up easy. **DO NOT** use a cleaning agent which contains bleach or ammonia as rather than removing the smell it intensifies it and the pup is more likely to be drawn back to the spot.
 Instead use either proprietary products available from good pet shops, equally good is biological soap powder or warm water with vinegar in it.

It is also useful to have a small cosy place in a busy room in the house i.e. Kitchen or living room. This is a place where pup can sleep during the day and where he is less likely to make a mess unless left for too long.

When you take him outside observe his actions closely and you will soon see what he tends to do just before he toilets. When you take him out you can give a command like '**Be quick**' or '**Hurry up**' just as he begins his preparations, then repeat again and praise when he '**performs**'. When the lesson is learnt you can find suitable places for him to relieve himself and not have him '**go**' when he should not.

As pup grows up so will his control develop and his ability to go longer without needing to relieve himself and you will know from early observation that it is time to go outside. This system works for old dogs, like rescues, who have never lived in a house, they should not need to go out every 1/2 hour or so as a pup would.

Finally if taught to '**go**' on command....

But just in case accidents happen always have a few poo bags with you and dispose of them responsibly.

NOTE - if you need to take the '**used**' poo bag back to the car to dispose of it then to avoid smell in your car use a plastic container with a lid (Vanish tubs are very good) half fill with cat litter and when placing the poo bag inside shake the container a little - this will activate the deodorant in the cat litter and mean no smells in your car.

Chewing - control

Fido Fact – DOGS CHEW

It is a fact of life that all puppies and some adult dogs chew. It only becomes a problem when they chew the wrong things like legs of furniture, carpets, cushions, slippers, walls and many other things.

Dogs will chew for many reasons, the most common and easiest to recognise is when the puppy is teething – as with a human child - this will happen. The provision of toys and redirection of his need from unsuitable things to his toys will often be enough.

'**Chew**' toys need to be:-
    suitable for the size of pup
    changed for larger one (s) as pup grows
    checked regularly for wear
    suitable for purpose

There are several good chewing toys produced by manufacturers; **KONG** is a good make who produce a range of suitable toys. Tennis balls are not suitable as 'household' toys as they tend to break up and could be eaten.

A good way to help encourage chewing the correct item is when he is put into his daytime safe place put his toy with him. Also when in the room with the family and he starts to chew something inappropriate give a fierce '**NO**' and encourage him to chew his **KONG**.
Stuffed toys are not safe for a chewer as the stuffing can be dangerous.

It is a little known fact that a dog may return to chewing at around 6 / 12 months as the adult teeth are setting and therefore always ensure that suitable chewing toys are available.

There are other reason why dogs will chew and they are often
symptoms of a more serious problem, this needs special attention and even professional help.

Jumping up

Let us first establish why your cute, loving bundle of fluff is jumping up in its adorable way and learn why this must be stopped as soon as possible and how to stop this unacceptable behaviour.

In the wild our wolf pup would require mum to feed it first with her milk and then it change to '**adult**' food i.e. raw meat. Like human infants this transition requires a phase of baby food. To do this the mother wolf regurgitates some of her partially digested food. When the pup jumps up and licks the mother's muzzle it is to trigger the regurgitation.

So, as you might have guessed, when your pup jumps up to lick your lips he is expecting you to regurgitate some food for him; the fact that human anatomy places our mouths are further away means that the dog has to jump up to illicit the delivery of food. A dominant dog is able to place its paws on the shoulders of a less dominant dog and when a dog is jumping up this is effectively what it is doing – exerting its dominance.

While the pup is small, and usually clean, and you are not in your best clothes jumping up might be acceptable. Imagine however the following scenario :- he is fully grown and covered in mud, you are in your best clothes, or worse your fussy aunt, this is not the time you want to be '**welcomed**' with your dog jumping up.
It is therefore vital that the jumping up behaviour is stopped before it becomes a problem.

Do Not Acknowledge the Jumping

To begin, whenever pup rushes to greet someone or be fussed, do not encourage or allow jumping up. Say nothing and move away even turning your back on pup. When his paws are all back on the floor give the signal / command for sit.
You will need to be persistent at first, but once pup sits, praise and reward, but then let him jump again push him down without

acknowledging him in any way. Very quickly pup will see that jumping up holds no reward and will decide not to repeat the action. In this way the behaviour is corrected **before** it could be linked to a display of dominance.

He already knows that jumping up is not acceptable behaviour.

LEAVE IT - command

A useful exercise, both in the house and outside is to have a command to be able to tell your dog what not to touch.

Start this exercise, sit on a chair with some choice treats and the dog sitting in front of you. Place a treat on your knee where the dog can see it, if your pup is too small to reach it then use a low coffee table or the floor. Keep the treat close by you and first keep your hand close enough to be able to grab the treat should he try to take it. Tell him '**Leave it**' as you place the treat down. What you want to achieve is that the dog makes no effort to take the treat.

At first he will probably try to do so, but you must grab the treat before him and repeat the '**leave it**' command. Repeat this two more times then stop, but repeat the whole exercise 3 or 4 times a day until the desired result is achieved.

When he makes no effort to take the treat, pick it up and give it to the dog saying '**There you go**', or something similar. Repeat several more times to ensure the dog understands.
Now when outside and the dog makes an effort to go towards something you do not want him to – a leaf – a cat – another dog – broken glass – say '**LEAVE IT**' and encourage him away.
When he does leave it and moves away – praise and give a treat, gradually phase out the treat and leave praise.

Some dogs will happily leave food or a toy in the home environment but find other things much more tempting in the outside world.
Therefore to increase the effectiveness of **LEAVE IT** continue to practice with different objects in different situations.
If your dog has a special toy or ball of high value, teach him to **LEAVE IT** rewarding if successful.

Remember to use the command whenever possible in the early days to ensure that the lesson is thoroughly learnt as failure to do so may cost your dog his life

HOME ALONE

A very important lesson for the puppy to learn is that it is OK to be left on its own and not to fret. This is a good lesson to teach in the first month when he cannot go out into the wide world.

Dogs are social creatures and prefer company rather than being alone, once they come to live with us they must be taught how to cope when we have to go out and leave them. If taught properly they should be quite confident at being left alone and know how to occupy themselves. This lesson correlates effectively with toilet training.

As with all aspects of training start small and develop slowly until the lesson is learnt. At first encourage puppy to play with toys that he can play with by himself. Suitable chew toys stuffed with a treat or a food dispensing toy like a **Kong** are very useful.
First encourage puppy to settle down in his confinement area i.e. crate / doggy play pen / kitchen / utility room, wherever he will be left at night or when we go out.

Give him his toy and a suitable command like 'Settle down and play' and then leave him to get on and chew / play while you get on with your chores.
Do not talk to him, just glance over casually to see how he is doing. If all is well quietly leave the room for a few seconds and return, do not make a fuss on departure or return, instead be very '**matter of fact'** about it.

Gradually increase the length of time you are gone and above all keep the whole thing calm.
You can also bring in the '**Settle Down'** lesson (**Section 6-12**) for short periods when watching TV as this will help prepare him for when you have to leave him.

When you are ready to try the first proper spell of separation, leave the radio playing quietly to take away the silence. Ensure that puppy has been out to relieve himself prior to confinement.
 In sight of puppy prepare his toys - it is good to have several toys of the type previously mentioned.

Place them in his area and shut the door with him outside - he will want to get in to the toys and treats. When he makes it clear that '**he wants in'** open the door letting him in and say '**settle down and play**'; then close the door and leave him.

Puppy will be busy trying to get all the hidden treats, the stuffing in the chew toy and the kibble in the Kong. Somewhere in all of this he will get tired and fall asleep. Make sure when you return that your return is calm and casual, turn off the radio open the door and take pup out to go to the toilet.

Do not make a fuss as you prepare to leave nor when you return; in fact encouraging pup to bring you a chew toy to receive fuss is excellent and avoids jumping up. Pretend to release a treat from the toy and give it to puppy, he will be so impressed.

Dogs generally sleep all night and all days have bursts of activity at dawn and dusk, it is during these periods that, when left alone, a dog may become vocal or destructive.

Leaving him with lots of stuffed toys etc. will occupy the departure in the morning and retrieving the toy upon your arrival will direct the dusk period.

When you are at home do not spend all your time with your dog, teaching him to settle down and occupy him-self while you do other things. This will make him more confident and able to occupy himself and less likely to suffer separation anxiety and the destructive habits of chewing and barking that accompany it.

Barking

Fido Fact:- Dogs bark!
It's just as natural as humans talking It only becomes a problem when the dog doesn't know when to stop. After all would you want your beloved Aunty around if she chatted all the time?

You do not want to stop your dog barking, just control when it barks. To do this we must understand why dogs bark, once you have identified the why then you can begin the training.

The dog barks excessively for any of the following reasons, in some cases there can be more than one reason.

- **Breed characteristics**
  Some breeds like terriers, hounds and guarding breeds have a predisposition to be vocal.

- **Playfulness and excitement**
  This starts as a puppy as a way to encourage someone to play with it. This can develop into barking in anticipation of anything it sees as being exciting.

- **Dominance**
  Staking out it's territory.
  Expressing its needs i.e., feed me now or let me out
  Displaying high status in the pack

- **Bad training**
  The owner has inadvertently rewarded bark
  Boredom, insufficient stimulus to mind and body
  Loneliness, insecurity, stressed or uncomfortable
  Improper socialisation
  Attention seeking

- **Danger**
  As a member of a pack it is ok to warn the leader of a potential danger, perhaps a strange person or sound; The dog should stop barking when the leader / alpha shows up.

Excitement Barking

This sort of barking is experienced when preparing to go for a walk or getting in to the car prior to arriving at the walk site. Your dog is

saying' Hey, were going for a walk! '**Are we there yet?**' , **'This is so exciting'**

This is a fairly easy lesson, although a little tedious for us.

If the dog starts the excitement barking in the house prior to the walk, you will need to show the dog that this sort of behaviour gets him nowhere.

Gather your things together as you normally would and observe your dog. As soon as he starts rushing about and barking **STOP** what you are doing and go and sit down. Do not say anything, do not remove coat, boots or whatever extra clothing you put on, just go and sit down quietly.

Initially this will confuse the dog, but eventually he too will settle down. After a few minutes get up and carry on as before, but immediately the dog starts barking go and sit down. Eventually the dog will learn that his barking does not get him what he wants.

If the barking occurs when travelling in the car prior to the walk, make several '**dummy**' runs that do not end up in a walk. For example up to the shops and he stays in the car (ventilated of course and not on a warm day). Also go to different venues so that there are no associations to trigger the barking.

Fido Fact   - Dogs have a better sense of smell, hearing and sight than humans. So just because you can't hear, see or smell anything doesn't mean there is nothing there, your dog knows better.

How to stop excessive barking.
First identify why your dog barks a lot and then make the necessary adjustments as listed below, before you start retraining your dog.

Dominance driven barking- look at how the dog views it's place in the   pack (your family) and adjust to lower it's status.

External trigger- perhaps a sound like a phone ringing or a door bell, a person who calls at the house or traffic. In which case desensitisation to the trigger can prove very effective.

Training error- acknowledge where you went wrong and start again.

Fido Fact – Your dog does not have a problem with its barking. It is you, your family and neighbours that have the problem!

NEVER reward your dog for barking, and **NEVER** commit the three dog training sins, when your dog barks **DO NOT**:-

1) Yell or scream at the dog- it gives attention which acts as a reward also the dog will think you are joining in and get more excited.

2) Let your dog in or out, feed it or play with it – again this rewards the dog for barking by doing what it told you to.

3) Cuddle, talk soothingly or give treats – this tells the dog you are happy with him and what he is doing.

Time for action
• Asses if dominance is a contributing factor and adjust home life.
• Remove what ever acts as a stimulant
• Avoid leaving dog alone for long periods if this causes barking. Then begin a programme of desensitisation.
• Give plenty of exercise both physical and mental, a tired dog is less likely to bark.

These methods are very effective for controlling barking, but this is not an easy problem to solve and the longer the dog has been barking the longer it will take to control it.

Speak and Quiet
A very effective way to re-educate a dog away from barking is to teach the dog to bark on command. Use the trigger that starts the dog barking and give the command speak and repeat this while the dog barks, praising the dog. No I have not gone mad!

After a few repetitions of this you give the command just before the trigger and when the dog barks again praise it. Now it's time to introduce a new command, quiet. After the dog has barked and it stops to draw breath or because the trigger has gone away give the new command and praise the dog.

Eventually the dog will understand that it must bark when you say speak and cease when you say quiet. If you never give the command to speak the dog will not bark.

Distraction
In some types of barking, especially if the problem is not well established this method can work well. If you know what sets your dog to bark then just before it happens distract the dog with a simple obedience command like **SIT**. Or a loud clap or whistle which causes the dog to look away from the trigger and focus on you, then reward the dog.

Desensitise the dog
This is very effective with sound related barking like the phone ringing or the door bell. Get someone to phone you or ring the door bell and your dog starts barking, turn your back on the dog and ignore it and of course do not answer the phone or door bell.

Eventually the dog will get confused and receiving no reward from you will stop barking, when it does wait a moment and if it is still quiet praise the dog. Keep repeating this several times a day for several days, after three weeks repetition with no barking from the dog the lesson is learned.

Ignoring the dog
Sometimes a dog barks to seek attention, if you acknowledge him in any way even to scold him he has got his reward. Instead turn your back on him and pretend he isn't there. Initially he will try harder, but if you carry on ignoring him he will stop.

When he does stop turn to face him and praise him. Repeat this lesson every time he barks for attention, and make sure to praise when he lies quietly beside you.

Section 6

Lessons

The Dog's world

A dog's world is full of fascinating sights, sounds and of course smells; and then there is us. To a dog, by comparison to that interesting sniff, we can be very boring. On a walk we stroll along often lost in our own thoughts, only paying attention to our dog when **HE** does something to attract **OUR** attention, like pulling, sniffing, in short being a dog.

As a trainer I am frequently told '**my dog doesn't listen to a word I say**'. In some cases it is because owners talk too much and the dog, who remember does not speak human, just switches off, as we would when Great Aunt Mavis comes calling; apologies to anyone called Mavis who is a great aunt.

However in most cases the dog is so distracted by all the interesting things around him that he basically forgets that we are there because we are not interesting.
If we want his attention then we need to '**up our game**' and become as interesting if not more so because of the competition.

In this competition, we need to start with small victories.

Remember me — Lesson 1

Equipment needed
The dog, the handler, a pocket full of choice treats, collar, lead,

Location
A place of low distraction like your garden. This is one occasion when you do not want to start the exercise in the house, otherwise you may end up with your dog staring at you while you try and watch your favourite TV programme. So keep this one outside.

Method

Take your dog, on the lead, out into the garden and simply stand there. Discreetly have a treat in hand, but do not show it to your dog. The dog does not need to be in any special position, SAY **NOTHING**, just let him do what he wants. The object to this is that whenever he looks your way you must **quickly** praise and reward with a treat. In this way he will learn that looking at you is a good thing to do.

All that you have to do is keep enough of your attention on him to make sure that you reward correctly - easier said than done, but focus, it is worthwhile.

The first few times may take a while, be patient. If after a minute or so the dog has not looked your way say nothing but move your feet and position slightly - it should attract his attention and be ready to praise.

Be careful on the timing of your praise in this exercise, you need to be giving your praise and reward within one second of him turning his head. Any longer and he will not associate the praise with his action you might even find you have rewarded the wrong thing.

A useful exercise is to watch your dog and how many movements he makes with his head in the time it takes for you to say one, one thousand.

That is approximately the one second you have to respond, so it is a useful idea to practice in your head whist watching your dog to develop your timing before you begin the exercise. A good guide is that you need to be starting your verbal praise as the dog begins to turn his head in your direction, thus by the time his head is looking at you the treat is there also.

As with all exercises repeat three times then take a break and   repeat 3 or 4 times a day. When your dog starts finding that you are more interesting than what is around him you can move to a new location gradually increasing the level of distraction.

You can also increase the distance between you, but always make haste slowly and if difficulties arrive go back a few steps and rebuild your progress.
There are also some games you can play with your dog to help you be more interesting than the world around your dog.

Calm down, it is only a walk
Also known as Red light / Green light training

A dog needs to learn as soon as possible that going for a walk is
pleasurable, but not as a reason to rush about and be an idiot. It is such an easy
lesson to teach providing you have a garden it can be started before pup can even go
out on walks. Therefore by the time he can go '**walkies**' he already knows to be calm.

Dogs learn to '**read us**' by observing our movements and body language – we are
very predictable.
Your dog will 'know' when you are about to take him for a walk and the excitement
thus builds up.
What needs to be taught is an acceptable way to cope with this and the pleasure
starts sooner.

Begin by putting on your coat, pick up his lead and prepare to go. As soon as pup
rushes about and gets excited, put down the lead and sit in a chair – yes coat and all.
He will think you have gone mad and after some '**faffing about**' he will settle calmly.

When he does, begin your routine again. Each time he gets excited, go back take the
lead off and sit down in the chair.
At the point of his excitement I usually say '**Oh dear**!' he will soon learn that means
you got it wrong.
The phrase can be used on other occasions when he is not doing what I want. Each
time he is calm I praise and say '**Let's go'.**

He will very quickly see that if we are to go outside I must behave calm and quietly;
this lesson includes not rushing about, leaping up or barking as these are
unacceptable.

When finally you can put your coat on, clip on the lead, pick up a toy and go outside
you can then play in the garden – **the reward**.

The Sit

"You do not have to teach your dog how to sit, he already knows that!"

What we have to do is to create a way of telling him when and where to sit and for how long.

Before starting this exercise you need to have decided on what command you will use to tell him to **SIT** and more importantly what your command will be to **'UN-SIT'** or release your dog.

The **'un-sit'** command is used to release the dog from a sit when you have no other command suitable i.e. heelwork, fetch etc.

One of the worst faults that can occur in dog training is when, by default, you teach your dog that he only has to respond to your command after the forth / fifth or even sixth time of repeating.

Having a dog that sits on the first command can save its life and could be a life saver. Decide on your two commands, keep them short and different then write them in the Commands section of this **Fido Fax**.

This verbal command will be the last link in the 'Sit' command chain and should be introduced only when the dog is ready, in this way you should be able to avoid the danger of having to repeat the verbal sit command

Remember do not use it until the dog is ready and you are sure of getting the correct response.

Sit — Lesson 1

Equipment needed
The dog, the handler, choice treats, chair, peace & quiet

Location
In the home in a quiet room.

Method
The chair is for you to sit on with treats for the dog within easy reach.

Take one treat and hold it by the dog's nose, saying **NOTHING.**

Allow the dog to sniff the treat and as he does slowly draw your hand back and over the dog's head. The nose will follow the treat and as the head goes back the hind quarters will automatically lower to the ground (the sit). Praise the dog and give him the treat.

Now use your '**UN-SIT**' word and encourage the dog to move out of the sit position.

Repeat this exercise **TWO** more times then stop and allow time for the dog to relax and think about what you have just done with him.

Repeat the same exercise three or four times a day for the next few days.

When your dog is consistently and reliably able to perform this exercise in different rooms in the house and away from distractions, then move out into the garden where there are more distractions, but still using the chair for yourself. When the dog does this consistently both inside and out you can move on to **lesson 2**.

Sit — Lesson 2

Location
In the home in a quiet room.

Once again in the house and away from distractions, sit on the chair holding a treat, then just as you give the signal with your hand give the verbal command **ONCE**. Praise and reward as before. Repeat this two more times then rest.

Repeat the full exercise 3 or 4 times a day and when the dog is responding correctly inside the house move the training outside as in **lesson 1**.

Gradually create a few inches distance between your hand (and treat) and the dog's nose. When he is responding correctly to this revised signal each time both in the house and outside then move on to lesson 3.

Sit — Lesson 3

Repeating **lesson 2,** but this time allow a slight pause between the verbal command and the hand signal. Your dog should now be responding to the verbal command without needing the hand to move, just hold it in front of the dog a few inches from its nose.

If the dog does not respond repeat the **HAND SIGNAL** not the verbal command.

Once the dog remains constant in its responses you can then begin giving the command standing up. Be prepared for the dog to see this as being different to when you are sat on a chair, after all you are now adopting a more dominant stance.

If your dog starts going wrong go back to **lesson 1**, but this time with you standing rather than sitting and without a verbal
command.

Some dogs seem to accept the change in position easily whilst others become confused, but going back a stage will usually get them back on course.

Once the dog is responding correctly each and every time with you stood up, hand in the signal position (but not moving) and with the verbal command you can move on to **lesson 4**.

Sit — Lesson 4

Remember we want the dog to sit quickly, to **ONE** verbal command, without a signal and then to remain seated until he is told to do something different.

The object is now to gradually to phase out both the treat and the need for the hand signal, whilst keeping the correct response from the dog each and every time with different levels of distraction around.

Remember every time you make the exercise more difficult start where there are no distractions and build up the level of distraction as the dog progresses.

Sit — Lesson 5

The objective now is to phase out the treat and to speed up the sit response.

When the verbal command and the stationary hand signal are given, count the time lapse between the command and the dog sitting. This time becomes the benchmark, from here on only give treats for sits within this time; as the sit becomes quicker the benchmark changes as a quicker response is expected.

Once you are getting fairly quick responses you can look to how long the dog sits for and move on to **lesson 6**.

Sit — Lesson 6

The objective now is to extend the length of the sit.

Start this exercise inside and as before move outside for more distractions when the dog is stable in the exercise inside.

Until now the dog has only been expected to sit to receive praise and a treat before being released. Now once the dog has sat for a moment praise can be given and the dog released. Gradually lengthen the time he sits before giving praise etc.

When your dog consistently will sit for 1 minute move on to **lesson 7**.

Sit — Lesson 7

The objective now is to extend create distance between dog and handler.

As before, start this exercise inside and move outside for more distractions when the dog is stable in the exercise inside.

Ask your dog to sit, when he responds praise and take one step away, return and praise, reward and release.

This exercise will develop step at a time, do not try too much too soon, some dogs get very worried when their handler moves away so watch your dog and work at his speed.

If he gets up he is telling you he is worried, do not tell him off simply return command the sit and go back a few paces slowing down until he is happy and confident again.

Down

Fido Fact - Dogs can lay down

The down is best taught once the dog responds to the sit with the hand signal. It is a useful control exercise which helps to calm an excitable dog. It can also be used as part of further exercises to enrich the dog's life whilst increasing your control.

The dog should lay down in the sphinx position i.e. On its belly, hind legs tucked under with front paws ahead not on its side with legs out straight. A less formal resting position can be taught later (**Section 6 - 11 Settle down**)

Lesson 1

Equipment needed
The dog, the handler, choice treats, chair, peace & quiet. Instead of sitting on a chair you might prefer to sit on the floor.

Location
In the home in a quiet room.

Method
As with the sit you will be giving a hand signal to get your dog to lay down and only add the verbal command when you know your dog will lay down to the hand signal. Use the same release command from the down as you did in the sit e.g. '**Go play**'.

Start in the house where there are no distractions with treat in hand. Again hold the treat close to the dog's nose and then slowly lower your hand, palm downwards, with the treat held between the thumb and third finger, until resting on the floor.

Your dog may follow the smell of the treat down with his nose and if you are lucky he may even lay down to get at the treat. As soon as he is down praise, reward and release.

However, your dog may also just stand and watch your hand, do not worry, just wait. The dog is now having to work out what he has to do to get the treat. He may try various actions which can include pawing your hand, nosing your hand, licking your hand, sitting plus many other possible responses.

You **MUST** say and do nothing. If the dog continues working at getting the treat wait as long as it takes, he will get there. However if he gets distracted or looses interest repeat the hand signal again.

If he keeps getting distracted or losing interest consider finding somewhere with fewer distractions, trying the lesson before he eats and choosing a more rewarding treat. Or perhaps he's tired?

For some dogs using a low object like a chair or coffee table and holding your hand & treat under that can help them get the idea. Once they have done it once or twice try it just in front of the object and then away from it..
Repeat this twice more and then as a lesson 3 or 4 times a day.

When you are getting the correct response each and every time without difficulty you can progress to lesson 2.

Down — Lesson 2
As with the sit you can now increase the level of distraction by repeating lesson 1 outside. When you have the same success outside move on to lesson 3.
Down — Lesson 3

Begin inside again and start to introduce the verbal command just before the hand signal, as we did with the sit. Gradually reduce the level of the hand signal and if the dog responds consistently well for a couple of days you can move on to lesson 4.
Down — Lesson 4

Once again go outside and repeat lesson 3.

Further development
As with the sit you can increase the length of time you keep the dog in the down and the distance you can move away from the dog. Remember do not rush the training, if the dog goes wrong go back a lesson or two and then gradually rebuild the level of difficulty.

Settle Down

Some dogs are naturally happy to just settle down and do nothing, even sleep, without being told whereas others are, by nature, very busy active dogs and they benefit by being taught to '**settle down'**.

Unlike the down, sit or stand, which is formal exercise where you expect the dog to hold the position until instructed otherwise, the
settle down means lay down in any position it likes, it may adjust position, scratch, roll over, sit up, lay down etc., but he has to stay where he has been told and be quiet.
It is like a magic '**off'** button and helps the dog understand that now is the time to relax, be quiet and not rush about. For example of an evening when you are ready to sit and relax or at mealtimes or when visiting a not so '**doggy'** friend or relative.

It is also useful out on a walk for the dog to settle down, for example when you meet someone and you want to stand and chat.
You do not want a dog pulling, jumping up or fussing around wanting to continue the walk.
There are many other occasions where a well mannered dog is appreciated by you as well as others around you.

Lesson 1

This is an easy lesson for the dog to learn and as always it starts in the house. You need a chair, some treats, your dog with collar and lead on, plus (just for you) a drink and something to read or watch on TV; the last two are optional, but as you will have very little to do you might as well enjoy your training time.

The best time to introduce this lesson is after exercise. Settle yourself with all the equipment around you. Place the dog's lead under your foot and hold the loop end in your hand. Say nothing to the dog, but pull the lead tight so the dog can feel the pressure, then wait.

The dog is not sure what you want and will try all his lessons and possibly new things to figure out what you want this time. You can enjoy your drink and read or watch TV - just keep the lead tight and eye on your dog and what he does.

Eventually he will lay down or throw himself down on the floor, once he is still and stops struggling praise and reward him and slightly slacken the lead.

If he tries to get up do not release him, when he stays down for a few minutes then you can praise, reward and release. As usual repeat this 3 / 4 times a day and keep him down a little longer each time.

Lesson 2

When your dog stops fighting the lead and lays down you can introduce the verbal command, I use **'Settle down'**, but you use what you like.

Use your command when you have just put the lead under your foot and just before he lays down. I usually point to the floor when I give the command so he knows where to settle down.

Gradually you can say the command a bit sooner as we want to reach the point where the lead is no longer needed and that he settles down where and when you say. You can increase duration of time before you release him to play.

Remember to gradually build up the time the dog is in the **'settle down'** and bear in mind his age and level of activity. This should become a relaxing pleasure not a task he does not like.

So when he is lying quietly, calmly praise him for being good. Eventually he will learn this is how to behave in the house.

Lesson 3

You are now ready to take the exercise outside, first to your garden and then out to other places. As before go back to basics and introduce the exercise as we did in the house.

When the dog will do it each and every time, bring it in when you stop, but do not sit down. Also go on visits to friends and use it as a training session.

Eventually he will understand that whenever you say '**Settle down'** he can lay down and relax.

Stand — Lesson 1

Equipment needed
The dog, the handler, choice treats, chair, peace & quiet.

Location
In the home in a quiet room.

This exercise is very useful when grooming or examining your dog.
It is taught in exactly the same way as the previous exercises.

Method
Start with your dog in the sit or down position. Hold the treat by the dog's nose with the palm of the hand facing towards the dog. Slowly draw the hand level and away from your dog, you may have to repeat the movement to encourage the dog to get up onto all fours.

Immediately he is up praise, reward and release giving your chosen command as used in the sit & down e.g. **'Go play'.**

Repeat the task twice more and as an exercise 3 or 4 times a day.

When the dog is responding correctly each and every time you can move on to **lesson 2**.

Stand — Lesson 2

You can now increase the level of distraction by repeating **lesson 1** outside.
When you have the same success outside move on to **lesson 3.**
If you have a small dog you can also teach this lesson on a table as it is useful when at the vets or grooming parlour as well as at home.

Repeat until you are getting the correct response each and every time, then move on to **lesson 3**.

Stand — Lesson 3

Begin inside again and start to introduce the verbal command just before the hand signal, as we did with the sit and down. Gradually reduce the level of the hand signal and if the dog responds consistently well for a couple of days you can move on to **lesson 4**.

Stand — Lesson 4

Once again go outside and repeat **lesson 3**.

Further development
As with the sit you can increase the length of time you keep the dog in the stand and the distance you can move away from the dog. Also introduce the idea of being handled and groomed whilst standing still.

Remember everything you add is a new dimension and keep it short, take it slow and if the dog goes wrong, gets confused or upset go back a lesson or two and then gradually rebuild the level of difficulty.

Heelwork

Having a dog walking happily by your side, on or off the lead, is every owner's dream. Whilst waiting for pup to be able to venture forth in the wide world after his injections owners have this vision of the two of them strolling, in harmony, down the lane across the field or through the woods enjoying nature or the pure joy of companionship.

Finally the day arrives, they venture forth and, oh dear, and from day one it has all gone wrong - the young pup doesn't know about the owner's vision, it is both excited and nervous of this brave new world and proceeds to rush about, pulling in all directions or just flattening into the ground and refusing to walk.

Very quickly a pulling match begins. The owner is frustrated and /or embarrassed and so the shouting begins. The command **'HEEL'** is said repeatedly accompanied by yanks on the lead. The owner thinks clearly the dog is stupid because it does not know what **'HEEL'** means or where he should walk.
He thinks the dog will soon learn if the command is spoken louder and accompanied by sharp yanks on the lead

If I gave you the command **'ROSEBUD'** would you know what I wanted you to do? Of course not so why should you expect your pup, a different species of animal, to understand English / German /or any other spoken language?

It does not take the pup long to learn to hate the sound of the word **'HEEL'** and not enjoy walks. Similarly the owner will be frustrated and not enjoying the walks either, after all being tugged about is not fun which ever end of the lead you are on.
 The end result of this is that the dog doesn't get enough exercise as walks get shorter or less frequent, he gets bored and behaves worse and/or he becomes destructive and eventually is got rid of, branded a "**problem**" dog.

The other route is that he is taken in the car somewhere for him to have a good run around and get it "**out of his system**."
Chances are he hasn't learnt to come when called, and the joys of running about are more interesting than his owner, so he won't come back, more frustration.

When finally he decides to return the owner in temper reprimands him for being so naughty, the dog thinks he is punished for returning and soon learns not to return, once again he is got rid of. All this could have been avoided with a little bit of time and the right training he can learn both to walk to heel nicely and to come when called, let's see how easy it is!

Walking with owner is fun

The object of this is like all aspects of reward based learning is to get the dog to think he is choosing to do he wants to do when in reality it is what we want him to do. A willing volunteer is worth ten pressed men. This lesson/game has multiple parts to it and all need to be started at the same time, but as separate exercises, then joined together later when ready. Each part to this lesson will be called an exercise for ease of reference, and can be started the day after your pup arrives with you. For those with a dog that has already learnt to pull see (**Section 7 - 5 The Pulling Dog**)

Exercise 1: I'm fun to be with
This is all about convincing your pup that you are the best thing since sliced bread and he wants to be with you. To that end, choose a toy which from here on is your toy. See **(Section 3-1 Equipment)**

This is soft, not too bulky and could fit in your pocket, start by playing with your toy when pup is around, and sell the idea this is fun! As he shows interest include him in the game but make sure you stop before he gets tired or bored and that you end it and retain the toy.
This can be repeated several times a day. Soon your pup will get excited to see you bring out the toy, success.

Exercise 2: Collars and leads are fun
This is a simple exercise designed to prepare the puppy for walking on the lead. First get the puppy use to wearing his flat collar, most puppies tend to scratch at their collar but do not remove it just try and distract them with play and food they will eventually accept it.

Once they are happy with their collar the lead can be attached and dragged about in the house, but keep an eye on pup to make sure he doesn't chew the lead or get caught on something.
Every time you clip on the lead give a command like "**Lead on**" and then give him a treat, he will soon see the lead as something good.

Exercise 3: Sit is rewarding

The sit can also be taught now as it will be needed later when we pull all these exercises together, see (**Section 6 - 5 Sit**)

Exercise 4: Catch me if you can

Before you begin this exercise you need to decide which side you want to walk your dog, most people tend to want their dog by their left leg, if you plan to do competition work or work to the gun they must be on the left. If you want your dog on the right simple reverse the leg directions.

We are aiming for the dog to be walking on a loose lead with it's shoulder level with our leg, this is called the **HEEL** position.

Begin this exercise in one room where there is space enough to move around, pick a time when puppy is not tired ideally just before a meal so he is hungry.
With some small, tasty, quick to eat treats, get pups attention and when he comes to you drop a treat by your foot on the side you wish him to walk and praise him when he eats it.
Take a step or two saying "**let's go**" or "**Off we go**" stop and drop another treat wait for him to find and eat it, each time he takes the treat praise him.

Repeat this three or four times then stop, fuss him and release to play.

This exercise can be repeated four or five times a day.

Within a few days to a week your pup should be getting the idea that all things good are to be found by you especially your left leg.

When he is staying with you easily you can include another room in the house, then when he is happy with that bring in the garden.
Be prepared there are more distractions so you may have to take a step back to when you first introduced this to pup and build up to where you were in the house.

Once your pup can sit on hand signal and/or verbal command, is happy with collar and lead and follows you about the house and garden you can move on to **Exercise 5 walking on lead**.

Exercise 5

If all has gone well by the time puppy has completed his injections & can go out into the world he should be ready to have his lead on and begin heelwork on a lead without pulling. To find out why dogs pull see (**Section 7 - 5 The pulling dog)**

Once puppy can produce his 3 sets of 5 step heelwork, with sits and is happy in collar and lead you can pull all these separate elements and take him for his first steps out in the world. Remember there will be lots of distractions outside that he has not encountered in the home so on no account allow him to pull.

I always start their early '**lead on'** exercises in the home, then the garden and then outside. Fortunately pups require very little formal exercise, so lots of little training sessions a day are better than one long walk.

With pup on the lead and the lead held in both hands at waist height and close to the body stand still, say nothing and do nothing except watch your pup. He will fuss, pull, tug, bite the lead and much more, but stay still, say nothing and do nothing.

Eventually he will either sit or lay down, it may take time, but be patient, it will happen and when it does praise him, give him treats and say "**Off we go**" or "**Let's go**" and take a step forward. He will probably rush forward, when he does – stop and repeat the exercise again.

Each time you repeat the exercise make the dog sit for longer.

Eventually, you will be able to take a step without fuss or pulling you can progress to two steps and proceed as before until he takes two steps, no fuss and no pulling. Increase to three then four steps and so on until he walks without pulling.

He has learnt the only way we go for a walk is without pulling or fussing.
If he subsequently pulls at all on the walk then stop & wait and when he sits then you set off again. He will also have learnt when you stop walking he must sit; this is great when you meet a friend you want to talk to.

When you and pup are ready and able to go outside then extend the '**in the house'** exercise by opening the door you will go through. Put the lead on and begin the exercise, but this time head to go out through the door.

As this is new it may encourage the dog to pull, in which case go back one step and get the dog to sit.

Repeat the exercise until you and he can walk in and out through the door without pulling. Include some walking in the garden, then open the gate and extend your walk training out into the driveway, lane or pavement.

Repeat several times a day and pup will soon walk without pulling. He is not yet walking properly to heel, but he is not pulling.

Now you can move on to improve his heelwork see (**Section 6 - 20**)

Developing heelwork

Going for a walk should be a pleasure for all concerned and so a little time spent when pup is young will yield a lifetime of reward.

A dog needs to be able to walk to heel in the correct position and on a loose lead to be safe when near traffic, around people or animals; indeed it is a legal requirement.

So far puppy has learnt that not pulling is the way to go, now we want him to walk orderly beside us on a loose lead and when off lead.

The following exercises will help the dog to understand what the heel position is and that we want him to keep in that position.

Small / fast breeds

The small breeds tend to be quick, speed is their natural way and owners often feel as if they are always playing catch up and that the dog's speed is a disadvantage when training. However you can turn this around and use their speed as an advantage.

Working small / fast dogs on circles challenges them more and by playing catch up on lead encourages them to work at being with you. Sits also slow them down, so rapid sits gives the owner more control and also calms the dog.

Try the **rapid-fire sequence**, begin with the pup sitting beside you, take one step and sit, praise and then repeat. See how many sits you can achieve in a given distance.

You can increase to **sit– 2 steps – sit** and again see how many can be achieved in a given distance. Working in circles slows the dog down especially when combined with these '**rapid fire exercises'**

Large / slow breeds

The larger breeds tend to be slower, some even 'day dream' so circles are of no use. Instead use long straight stretches and avoid too many sits as they find these tedious and can slow them down.

When you set off to walk, give the command with a brisk, uplifting sense of energy and then move off rapidly – this encourages the dog to speed up more and keep up with you.

Hurry up & Go slow

Changes in speed are an excellent way to improve heelwork and sits. Dogs can get bored very quickly when walking to heel and boredom leads to bad behaviour so keep them on their toes and concentrating on you rather than other things.

You will need two commands, one to go faster and one to slow down. Remember it does not matter what the word used is just be consistent. To speed up the word could be:- Hustle / quickly / fast and to slow down it could be :- **Steady / slow**. I use '**Hustle' and 'Steady'.**

When walking in a safe place suddenly give the command to speed up and move off brisk enough to leave your dog behind, he will have to rush to catch up, when he does praise him.
Similarly give the command to slow down and return to normal speed, later give the slow down command and walk as slowly as you can.

 Repeat these throughout your walk and he will soon be focused on you having learnt '**Boy he / she is tricky, I better keep my eye on you'.**

You can then vary your speed, like changing gears in a car, normal to slow, to fast, to slow, etc. First give commands before '**changing gear**', later drop the command and just do it.

Twist & turn
You can now use your slow down command to teach the dog how to turn left and right. With the dog on a loose lead, and with treat in hand, get the dog's attention with a toy in the left hand, when ready to turn right (away from the dog) say '**Fido Steady'** and lead the dog around to the right with the toy.

When the dog turns with you, praise and play with the toy; repeat 2 more times and then leave & repeat later in the day.

For the left turn, which is more difficult as you are stepping towards the dog, you will need the toy in the left hand and lead held loosely in the right.
Give the command '**Fido, steady'** and use the toy to guide the dog through the right turn, praise and play with toy.

Once your dog can make left and right turns easily you can return to your '**catch me if you can**' exercise.

With the dog on a loose led, holding the loop in hand by your waist give the command for heelwork '**Fido, close**' and set off without warning turning right, go in circles, go straight, stop, go fast, go slow.

The idea is to get your dog to fight to be with you and pay attention when out and about. Offer praise when the dog is with you in the **HEEL** position.

When beginning the exercise do only short spells then sit, praise and play.

Gradually increase the length of time in the '**Twist & Turn'.**

Remember keep it fun, if the dog thinks it is a game he will enjoy

laying it so you must believe it first.

Happy Heelwork!

Stay/Wait

There are many reasons why a dog owner should teach Fido to
Stay or **Wait**.
- A dog or person in the distance to which Fido may run.
- Wait when getting out of the car.
- Wait before going through a door or gate.
- Something dangerous ahead such as a road.
- Wait before eating

Stay & Wait – why are there two similar commands?

Stay is often used to say to Fido "Stay there until I come back to you" In other words you would normally not call your dog over if you'd asked him to Stay.

Wait is usually used to say to Fido, "**wait by the gate until I tell you go through it**", or "**wait there and I'll call you over**".

Wait is used before a command to do something.

Saying all that often people choose one command and use that for everything as people do get confused as to which to say when.

I prefer to use a single command to avoid confusion.

Teaching Fido to Stay/Wait

There is a fairly easy way to teach these commands and a more difficult route which seems to have almost become the norm.

The easy way – show Fido what to do

Attach your lead to Fido and follow the steps below:

Training alone:

Place the handle of your lead over something to stop Fido wandering off. Use one of those corkscrew metal dog tethers that screw into the ground, a thin but strong stake or even a garden spade or fork dug in deeply using the handle to place the lead over.

Step 1: Get Fido used to being left behind. Say to Fido "**Stay or Wait"** in a low calm but clear voice **ONCE,** turn your back on him and walk a few steps away.
He may try to follow and be straining on the lead. Go back to him and praise / reward. Repeat this a few times.

Step 2: This time ask Fido to Sit first then repeat as above. Take a quick glance behind and if he is no longer sitting then walk back and ask him to Sit again. Repeat a few times.

Step 3: If all is proceeding well then try increasing the distance you walk away from Fido and even try walking around him in a circle.

Step 4: When happy that Fido understands what he is doing, take the lead off the tether but leave on Fido. Lay the lead next to your tether and repeat the Stay process.

If you have a Helper

As with **Training Alone** but this time your '**Helper**' acts as a sort of human post.

Keep Fido's lead on but lay it on the ground behind him.

Ask your helper to place a foot firmly on the end of the lead and stand behind Fido. It is important that your helper does not interfere with the dog in any way.

Repeat the '**Stay or Wait**' command turning and walking away as before.

Your helper should get a "**feel**" that Fido is not going to move and can gradually take their foot off the lead and step backwards.

Repeat this process increasing distances and even trying to walk around Fido in a big circle.

Success! - Fido is staying alone!

The Recall

This is probably the most worrying of all lessons and after pulling, it is the one thing that really irritates most dog owners.
If you have a puppy then do not let it off lead other than at home until you are fairly confident that it will come to you.
It is better the dog never learns not to come when called.

If you have an older dog that has already learnt that he does not have to come when called then use a flexi-lead until the correct
action can be taught.

There are three principles the dog must learn that:-

1.   It actually wants to be with you
2.   it is always good to come to you when called
3.   you are always in control regardless of distance between you

You will have already learnt the **'Handlers are fun to be with'** lesson and to help the idea along whenever you are going to feed your dog call his name / or whistle, when he gets to you praise and give him his food.
The same goes for treats, make him work for fuss, food & treats.

NEVER chase after your dog, if he does not want to get caught, he will always win this 'game' of chase.

Recall — Lesson 1

Equipment needed
The dog, the handler, choice treats, chair, peace & quiet and for you to have decided what verbal command you will use.

Location
Begin in the home in a quiet room, and only progress outside when you are consistently getting the correct response each and every time.

Recall — Lesson 1 continued

Method
You must sit on the chair, with legs slightly apart, and the treats easily accessible in a pocket.

Encourage the dog to sit in front of you.
When he sits in the desired position give the verbal command for the recall :-
i.e. **COME** and immediately praise and reward.

DO NOT RELEASE THE DOG

Repeat this twice more and on the third time **RELEASE** your dog. Then as a lesson repeat the exercise 3 or 4 times a day.

When you are getting the correct response each and every time without difficulty you can progress to **lesson 2**.

Recall — Lesson 2
Sit on the chair as in lesson 1, this time call your dog to you using the verbal recall command and using a treat to help position the dog correctly, then praise, reward and release

Repeat this twice more and then as a lesson repeat the exercise 3 or 4 times a day. When you are getting the correct response each and every time without difficulty you can progress to lesson 3.

Recall — Lesson 3
Repeat lesson 1, but this time with you standing up, legs slightly apart. With the dog sat in front of you give the verbal command, praise, reward and release.

Repeat this twice more and then as a lesson repeat the exercise 3 or 4 times a day. After a few days, still in the house, assume the position, with treat in hands give his name and the verbal command to your dog while he is in the room with you, praise, reward and release.
 Continue practicing and after a few days try it with the dog in a different room.

To help develop this lesson, every meal you can recall the dog to you and then put his feed down. When you feel ready move on to **lesson 4**.

Recall — Lesson 4

Now try the recall outside, your garden is ideal, if you have one and if it is secure. Start by repeating **lesson 3** a few times and gradually extend the distance between you and your dog.
When you are getting the correct response each and every time you can develop the lesson further.
 Begin touching his collar before you give the treat.

Further ways to develop the lesson

So far the level of distraction has been limited, now it is time to convince the dog that in all locations it is always good to come to you when called. Enlist the help of a friend, find a safe place and release your dog.

In front of your dog give a treat to your friend, while you move a short distance away, call your dog. He may be reluctant to leave them and the treat. They must ignore him, you must make yourself interesting. When finally he gives up on them and comes to you, praise, hold collar and have your friend pass the treat to you and you then give it to your dog. He will soon learn that all good things come from you.

Always call your dog in a jolly happy voice and praise him profusely, however slow he was.

Always make it worth his while coming to you, fuss, treats or play.

When your dog is enjoying his run about call him back on a number of occasions, praise reward, release, touch his collar and give a treat.
In this way he will never know which time is the time to **'end his freedom'**

Always make returning pleasurable and progress slowly. Never show him how frustrated you are if it goes wrong, just stop, go away and consider how to change things.

Further ways to develop a good recall

Choose a toy which is lightweight, easy to tuck into a pocket and suitable for your dog - knotted ropes are ideal. This is to become **YOUR** toy, not his, but being a super nice Alpha you may allow him to play with it with you.

Time now to get a bit silly, sit on the floor or a low stool and play with your toy. Toss it into the air, shake it, have a party and make it so interesting that he wants to join in.

Allow a little play together, then stop the game with a suitable command, I use "**Game Over**", and make sure that **YOU** have the toy.

Repeat this several times a day, but always with you in control and your toy.

Now in the home do your recall and when the dog sits in the correct position reward and praise, then bring **YOUR** toy out for a short play.
Repeat this several times a day as with all training.

By now, both in the house and in the garden, you should be able to call your dog's name and the recall command and have a happy dog sitting in front of you ready for a touch of the collar, praise and reward.

It is now time to go where there are slightly more distractions, but do not be too adventurous too quickly.
If you are at all unsure use a long lead to start with, then you will still have control.

A few points to remember once you reach this stage:-

- Only give **ONE** command
- Never show anger or annoyance, however difficult he has been
- Always be delighted to have him close by you
- Do lots of recalls when your dog runs around off lead and
- always have a treat to reward the returning behaviour
- Every time your dog comes to you take hold of the collar to praise and reward. Then on that one occasion where he goes on lead and he thinks fun is over a little play with **YOUR** toy will soften the blow.
- If touching the collar is part of every recall, then he will not associate it with the end of fun.
- Never chase after him, if he starts being difficult, turn and walk away. Get out your toy to play with and ignore him, he will come around. Contact me for help.
- Always remember if there are lots of distractions then a high quality treat is needed.

If things don't seem to be going too well
Make Fido *want to come back*

"Fido doesn't listen anymore" or *"Everything was going well with his recall and then suddenly he changed".*
These are common statements made by dog owners every day regarding their dog's ability to come when called.
A good recall is essential for any dog owner to prevent getting into trouble. The modern dog owner is faced with a whole array of hazards when exercising their dogs. Joggers, cyclists, horse riders, ramblers, non-doggy people, other dogs, vehicles, livestock, and wildlife the list is seemingly endless...

Understanding your particular breed of Fido is a good place to start.

Working dogs bred for hunting prey or flushing game will have a strong prey drive.

This unfortunately can then over-ride everything else.

 Some breeds don't really care about hunting but would rather wander off to see the rambler in the distance or that other dog they can see.
Establish a good recall as soon as you get your puppy or dog.

The usual command is "**Fido** (your dog's name) **Come!**"

Some golden rules:

- If Fido is ignoring you when called **DO NOT** keep shouting or whistling. Use one of the following methods below. Initially Fido may come back if a strong voice tone is used but this is not a long term, reliable method. It may only work for one person in a family or very often Fido ceases to be "**scared**" by it!
- Change direction. Turn your back on Fido saying **"bye"** and walk away (only if safe). Continue changing direction as soon Fido catches up or runs past you.
- Try to keep Fido within a certain distance that you are
  comfortable with.
- Use a whistle. The Acme range of whistles are proven and
  reliable. The **Acme 210** is often called the recall whistle.

Ask Fido to "**come**" quickly followed by a rapid series of whistle pips.

- If Fido has already taken to running away in certain places or ignoring you stop the behaviour straight away. Put him on a lead in those places and go back to the garden or enclosed space to repeat the recall training. Try him again in the places he was "naughty" and see if there is an improvement.
-

  Don't allow Fido to hunt or find his own entertainment when off lead

Here are some tips for success:

- Start in the house making sure Fido is reliably coming when called.
- Use treats to begin with but try and alternate with praise so that Fido is not expecting a treat every single time. We want him to come to please you nor because there is food!
- Use the "**bear hug**" posture. Squat down facing your dog with welcoming arms outstretched when calling your dog. You will be less intimidating to Fido and more appealing.
- Make recall a game, fun! Call him between two, three or more people. Reward and use lots of enthusiastic praise such as **"Good Boy," "well done," "clever dog!"**
- Play hide and seek. Owners hide around the house or garden calling Fido. Again lots of praise.
- Continue the hide & seek games outside in the garden or an enclosed area.
- Another good recall game for treat driven dogs is to throw down a treat so that Fido can find it and whislt he is munching on that one the owner darts away calling or whistling.
  When Fido comes over repeat and so on.

Daily walks

- How to stop your dog from running off

All dogs need a little **'dog time'** each day – that chance to sniff, mooch around and do **'dog'** stuff.

What we do not want is the dog running off and finding things that are fun to do without us.

Having discovered this new fun he will make a regular habit of running off. Whilst he is off freelancing he can get himself into trouble, for example chasing sheep (which could lead to him being shot) or perhaps running across the road and causing an accident.

The better option is to teach your dog to stay around you, to show that all that is rewarding or fun happens close by you.

The best time to start this is before the dog learns what is out there, this can be started as soon as you realise that you have a problem and that you want to deal with it.

To complete the training you need a broad collar, unless you have a strong dog that does not walk to heel, in which case a harness will be better. You will need to deal with your dog's poor heelwork, but that is a separate lesson. (**See section 6-15**)

In addition, for this lesson you will need a long lead, if your dog is young then choose a lead to cover for when he will be fully grown.

You will also need lots of treats, and I do mean lots of treats, those treats need to be really tasty treats to begin with, later you can drop back to a lower grade of treat.

Do not waiver now from this routine until the lesson is fully learnt, this can take up to six months. During this period **DO NOT** let your dog off lead to run free.

Begin in the home, teaching the recall lesson as part of the training, then when the dog is coming to you reliably in the home you can bring it in on the walk.
(**See section 6-23**)

Pick a place to start this training and keep this place for your free walking exercise, until the dog is behaving correctly. By keeping to the same place for this lesson the dog begins to expect to do it each time you go there. We use that to our advantage and later we take the lesson to other locations.

It is also useful to teach the '**leave it**' exercise (**see section 2-11**) as these will all be used during this free walk period.

The first part of this exercise is to get your dog to watch you so in short if he looks at you he gets a treat.

Do not be tempted to call his name, but if he is too busy looking at other things and has not looked at you for about 2 or 3 minutes then try making a move, if that does not work try making a funny noise.

Have the treat in your hand ready so as soon as he looks at you give the treat and praise.

Gradually the dog will get the idea that it is worth his while looking at you.

Success! Now when you arrive at the site of your free walking exercise and he has sat by your side for equipment changes, then give your command to commence free walking – not that he will understand yet – and walk on.

I use the command '**let's go**' this command will be used often during these sessions and soon the dog will link the command with an action.

Lesson 1

The first objective is for the dog to learn he may only go as far as the length of the flexi-lead usually about 16 ft., some are longer. We also want him to see that it is good for him to look to you often and keep an eye on what you are doing.

So as you walk along keep an eye on your dog and have a treat in your hand. Whenever he looks at you offer him the treat, **DO NOT** call him to you; he must chose to return. When he does treat & praise then release with the free-walk command & walk.

If he gets to the end of the lead say '**NO, too far**' and give a small tug, if he responds by waiting for you, or returns to you, praise him. If he ignores you say '**Bye, Bye**', turn and go the other way. He will follow and when he catches up to you, praise, give treat and resume original direction.

When your dog has started to grasp these points, you can ask a little more of him and move on to the next lesson.

Lesson 2
Now bring in your '**No'** command when he starts to head off in the wrong direction and add '**Bye, Bye'** with its change of direction.

You can also use your '**Leave it'** command if he is following a scent line or into anything he shouldn't be.
Continue to reward with treats and praise every time he looks at you.

When he is trotting about happily without pulling on the long line and regularly looks to you and is getting his reward you can then move on to the next lesson.

Lesson 3
When at home your dog will now come to you every time you call him, you can include this in your free-walk training.

Now when he looks at you call his name / whistle and offer the treat & praise. Continue using your '**NO too far – leave it'** as needed. After about a week or so and if your dog is coming on command you can move on to the next lesson.

Lesson 4
Now when you call your dog to you, make him sit, hold his collar and give him the treat & praise. Then release command and walk on.

When this is progressing well begin to vary when you call him and when you just reward for looking at you.

Lesson 5
It is now time to take this training to a new site. Expect your dog to not get on well because this is a new site and he has no association here as he did in the old site.
Go back to earlier lessons and build up steadily as before.
When he has learnt his lesson here and is working as before move to a new site and start again.

Each site will get easier and when he will work well straightaway at a new site you are ready to move to the next lesson.

Lesson 6
Return to your original site and start to make yourself and the walk more interesting then involve the dog in '**your**' game.

Take a toy, perhaps a ball or whatever he likes to play with.
When he is up ahead still on the long lead, drop the toy close by you but in clear sight.

You now need to behave as you would if you had actually lost the toy and cannot see it.
Time for some good acting :-

'**Oh I've lost my ball / toy, where is it?**'

Encourage your dog to 'find it' then when he does, praise him, get him to bring it to you & reward with praise and a treat.

This can be repeated a few times on each walk and use the same command, i.e. '**Find it /Seek it**' or whatever you like, just be consistent.

Gradually make the finding exercise more difficult by using long grass, lumps & bumps, logs – anything to encourage your dog to work for it.

When your dog is searching for toys, trotting along happily on each new site, coming when called and not pulling, you can move on to the next and last lesson.

Lesson 7

It is now time to test the dog and see if you have been successful in your training. Return to the original site (assuming that it is a safe & secure site).

Proceed as before for 2 days of exercise then on day 3 towards the end of the free walk session call your dog to you and just slip the flexi off his collar and carry on as if it was still attached.

If all goes well you can repeat this pattern for the rest of the week gradually increase the amount of off lead work, but keep being interesting.

If this has gone well go to your second site and repeat what you have done this week and then on to the next week and next until you are able to walk your dog off lead without him running off.
But keep up the activities like searching for a toy, retrieves or anything else you can think of.

If the worst happens at any point and he runs off, return to the old pattern on the long lead and give it a bit longer to sink in.

The Retrieve

Whereas the retrieve is not as essential to a pet dog as it is to a working gundog or when taking part in competition, obedi-ence is still a very useful skill for your dog to learn.

Retrieving provides good exercise and mental stimulation and is a fun game for owner and dog to play together.

There are, of course, a few rules which must be obeyed:-

- You always end up with the retrieve item
- You never chase after the dog to try and take the retrieve item from the dog.
Failure on your part to observe these rules can lead the dog into thinking that **HE** controls the game, and you, and therefore that he is Alpha.

If taught well this need not happen and all the benefits can be gained.

Before you begin the exercise you will need:-

- A retrieve item
- Treats
- **TWO** verbal commands, the words chosen are not crucial provided that they mean something to you and that you are consistent in their use.

The first command will be used to instruct the dog to go and pick up the object, for example:- fetch, find, get it; personally I use **'hold'.** The second command is for the dog to give up the item to you once he has retrieved it, here words like **'give'** or **'drop'** might be chosen, or **'dead'** for a working gundog.

Teaching this lesson is easy and as always begins in the house and moves outside into environments which are more distracting when a 10 out of 10 accuracy in an area is achieved.
The method may seem a little backwards, but it really does work if taught correctly.

Lesson 1

The object of this lesson is for the dog to learn to sit happily in front of you with the retrieve item in its mouth and then release it on command.

I always begin teaching new lessons sitting on a chair because with some dogs the first few lessons can take a while. Once they are responding correctly then I can discard the chair and stand with legs slightly apart.

Sit upon the chair with your legs slightly apart, treats in an easily accessible pocket and the retrieve item (**RI**) in hand.
Show the dog the treat and then put it in your pocket, now hold the **RI** in front of the dog and wait. **DO NOT SAY ANYTHING** at this point.

The dog now has to work out what you want it to do, so he will try a range of actions, often going through all the skills you have taught and many you have not.

This will probably include sniffing & licking the **RI,** still say nothing and do nothing but wait.

In some cases you may need to show him the treat again to remind him what is up for grabs.

When he eventually takes hold of the **RI**, praise him, let him hold it for a second then offer the treat which he gets once the **RI** is given up.

 Do not worry if he '**spits**' the **RI** out to get at the treat, that can be dealt with later. Repeat the exercise two more times and then repeat the lesson 3 / 4 more times each day.

When the dog sits in front of you, takes the **RI**, holds it and gives it up for the treat each and every time you can now move on to **lesson 2.**
If however he shows no interest at all in the object an alternative method is given at the end of this section.

Lesson 2

Sitting as before show the dog the treat and present the **RI** and as the dog moves to take the object give the command for the retrieve, i.e. '**Hold**'.
When he takes the **RI** praise him and with one hand under his jaw praise for a minute then get out a treat and offer it to the dog, then as you see him begin to open his mouth give the   release command .i.e. '**Dead**', praise and reward.

Repeat this 2 more times and then the lesson 3 or 4 times a day.
When the response is consistent, each and every time, you can repeat the exercise with you standing up.

Lesson 3

From here the lesson now starts to look more like what you expect from a retrieve. Stand with legs slightly apart, show the dog the treat and return it to your pocket. Drop the **RI** just in front of you and give the retrieve command.
The dog should pick up the **RI** and sit in front of you, in which case praise, give the release command, praise and reward.
As usual repeat the exercise and lessons and when the accuracy is right each and every time you can then start increasing the distance the **RI** is tossed and then start phasing out the treat, but always praise.

The reluctant retriever
If you have a dog that is not very interested in the **RI** and just sits and looks at it and may be prepared to sniff or lick it , but not to hold it, one of the following suggestions may help to encourage him:-

1. If the **RI** is hard, try covering the mouthpiece in fake fur or closely bound string.
2. Praise and reward him for sniffing or licking the **RI** and then encourage him to see if there is merit in getting interested in the object. When he is happy to sniff, you do not reward for sniffing, expect more, perhaps a lick and then the hold.

3. Using an old cloth glasses case put really smelly treats - like dried liver or pieces of cheese, inside. Alternatively a piece of cotton / man's handkerchief with the treat tied into a knot in the corner. Show the dog one of the treats then return it to the case.

    Drop it on the floor and wait, again if he noses it then praise, pick up the case and remove a treat and give it to the dog.

    Gradually reward as the dog progresses from nosing, to picking up and then return to the training system, but continue using the case until he sees the fun.

It is important to remember that the praise and reward is essential to developing this exercise and especially so for the reluctant retriever.

Possible problems after the lesson has been learnt

Retrieve item brought back but not given up.
When the dog returns to you, do not try to take the item, create a new game - either take hold of the collar or put on the lead.

Throw another **RI** where the dog can see it, then give the command to release, when he does remove the restraint and send to fetch.

Repeat 3 or 4 times, then once he has the idea of how the game goes, then throw the **RI** get what he holds but do not send, you pick the item up.

Consider what has changed in his life - feed - his developmental stage (age) - his position in his family / pack.
Amend as necessary and return to basics to reinforce the lesson.

Bring a further extension to the game in that not all retrieves are his, some are yours.
Do it randomly so he never knows which becomes the end of the game.

"Retrieve item picked up, dog comes part of the way back then runs off to extend the game"

Never chase after him, do not get cross, walk away and always have 'your toy' (**Section 3-1 Equipment**).

Bring it out as you walk away and play with it. Be more interested in your game than him and his game.

He will return, do not be in a hurry to include him. Finally notice that he is there, make him give up the **RI** he had. Put the lead on and play with him and your toy to show that it was worthwhile him giving up the **RI.**

When at home consider any changes in lifestyle - feed - developmental stage (age) - his position in the family /pack and amend. Return to basics and incorporate a long training lead or long line / lead so that he cannot run off and make it more fun to bring the **RI** back to you than to keep it to himself.

Games we can play

In the wild all day long a dog has to hunt for his food and solve problems.

When he comes to live with us he has his food handed to him, quite literally 'on a plate' (in a bowl), and nothing to do but sleep - and they say:-

"it's a dog's life"

Seriously, however attractive that may sound to us, to a dog (wolf) that is an active breed it is **HELL**.
Teaching him games, or tricks and making him work for his food will provide the stimulation he requires to keep him happy and healthy.
It will make walks more interesting for you and your dog plus it is less likely that your dog will develop behavioural problems brought about by boredom.

While away the hours
This is a great way to entertain your dog in the home, especially when you have to go out. I
nstead of giving him 2 meals a day of dried kibble which is gone in the blink of an eye, put the kibble in a suitable hollow rubber toy—'**Kong's**' are ideal.

Remember what is a suitable size for a puppy will need to change when he gets bigger.

The object is that once you place the kibble in the Kong and place it on the floor, the dog nudges the Kong causing it to roll.
The dog can play with it as a moving toy, but it also allows small quantities of kibble to fall out of special holes. Thus the dog has both mental stimulation as he finds out how to get the food out, and exercise as it works at it.

Go fetch
The retrieve is a great way to exercise your dog and can provide fresh challenges by the terrain you are walking over.

Retrieve is taught initially as a formal exercise, but it is best used as an exercise game whilst out on a walk providing the situation is safe.
(**See Section 6 - 40 The Retrieve**)

Remember the same rules apply out on the walk as in the formal training environment, never chase after the dog to get the toy back.
Never shout or show anger when the dog does come back eventually, go back to basics and correct what **YOU** did wrong in the training.

Always make sure that when the game will be over that there is something else good for the dog to go on to, i.e. a treat.

Hide & seek
This is a great game to encourage the dog to use his natural instinct to hunt.
The game can be played in the house, garden or when out on a walk if the area is suitable and safe.

The game is best started in the house and can then be moved outside as well when the lesson has been learnt.

To start the exercise use treats, either put your dog to sit, or if he does not know that exercise yet have someone hold his collar.
Show the treat and then go to different places in the room and pretend to hide the treat, rub a bit of treat to scent each spot and then make sure the treat is not the last place you pretend to hide it in.

Return to your dog and command the dog to search for the treat, you can use whatever command you like, the most common are:- '**find, seek, hunt**', - I use '**lost**'.

At first you will need to encourage the dog and like a child generally help him along, taking him to each place you went, he should smell where you rubbed the treat, as he sniffs give the search command e.g. **Find / seek**.

 When you reach the place where the treat is hidden repeat the command in the same voice as before, several times and praise the dog when he finds the treat.

Repeat this several times until he gets the idea of the game.
Gradually you can reduce the amount of commands given and the level of your involvement and the dog will do all the work.

When the dog has learnt the game you can then substitute his favourite toy instead of the treat, repeat the exercise, praise him and play with him with the toy. Offer him a choice of a treat in exchange for the toy. Once the retrieve is taught it will link into this exercise, but remember do not rush to take the toy off him, let him enjoy it a little first.

When he is working well looking for his toy in the house, you can then move into the garden and play the game in the same way with the toy.
Finally take the toy, or a ball, out on your walks and then, in a safe and suitable place, you can play the game.
This can be done even if your dog is not ready to be off lead it can be done with the dog on a long line / lead.

Eventually when the dog is able to be off lead you can quietly drop a ball in long grass and then send your dog to find it.
If you travel by car to get to the start of the walk then leave him in the car when you get there, drop balls around in the grass and then get the dog to hunt for them.

Track me if you can
In this game the object is to get your dog to follow a scent track until he finds a toy or person; it is great fun for tiring the kids as well as the dog.

The game needs to be '**played**' in a safe area where there is plenty of space with trees and bushes.
If you have a child with you put the dog to sit, show him his toy and send the child off with the toy and instruct them to scuff their feet on the ground and not walk in a straight line.
They need to go about 30 / 50 yards then hide and wait.

You may need to encourage the dog to follow the scent trail with the command **'TRACK ON'** until he finds the child with the toy.
Praise him and give him the toy and play with him.
Repeat several times until the dog gets the idea, remember do not take the same track or use the same hiding place each time, that would be predictable.

If you do not have a child, then leave the dog in the car and put the toy out to be found. Scuff your way out and back then collect the dog and proceed as before.
If you have a friend, or partner that walks with you then they can hold the dog while you walk out and hide the toy and walk back.

Once the dog has learnt to track, you can set longer scent trails and more difficult hunting patterns to challenge the dog and make him think.

Section 7

Behavioural Issues

Behaviours we do not want

There are many qualities in dogs that we love, companionship, love, loyalty, their working skills (e.g. scenting / retrieving abilities) and the pleasure they give.

However there are some aspects we do not want and the sooner we recognise these and deal with them correctly the easier it is.

But remember:-

a dog is a dog, is a WOLF

In some cases it is how we respond to his natural behaviours that can make a bad situation worse or even create the problem ourselves.

The following section gives some guidance as to how to tackle a problem when it first appears, but if you are not getting any improvement after a week or two consult a professional trainer or behaviourist for help.

Feed and its effects

When a person is choosing what to feed their pup, the first consideration is **'What should I feed?'**

They then consider the age and possibly the breed of their dog often starting with what the breeder suggests, a decision based on online research, a friends' recommendation or the advice of the local pet shop.

A few may consider what work their dog will be doing.

Of course what we all want is a food that is:-

- easy to obtain
- easy to feed
- good for the dog keeping him fit and healthy
- perhaps with a variety of flavours so that he does not get bored eating the same thing every day
- Cost - within our budget

We all accept that with humans **'We are what we eat'**, but rarely do we consider that maxim with our dogs; so let us take a moment to consider our dog's diet.

The truth is that many of the **'unwanted'** behaviours may not be due to Fido being a bad dog, but due to him being on the wrong food – a bit like a hyperactive child being on artificial colourings.

Dog owners today are faced with a formidable array of foods all claiming to be the best for their dog.
Pet superstores offer a vast selection of food ranging from familiar old school brand names through to Raw, Gluten Free and most recently Grain Free foods.

Add into the confusion, breed specific foods, Working Breed, Light, Senior and Junior diets!

Many dogs do alright on the food they eat, but some do not.

Even the best food is no good if it does not agree with you; for a person with a dairy allergy milk becomes a poison.

Think of children and **'E'** numbers.

So how do you know if your dog's food is not right for him?

Ask yourself these questions as the answers may point to a problem with the feed:-

- Is the coat looking good, does it shine? If not there is a problem. (poor ingredients)
- Is he low on energy or too high? (protein too high or low, poor quality)
- Is he too fat or thin? (overfeeding wrong diet, too little food, poor quality)
- Is the skin flaky? (allergies, quality of food)
- Is there evidence of excessive hair loss (allergies, wrong diet for breed)
- How is his general health, does he suffer from recurrent digestive problems. (quality, ingredients)
- How are the motions both by way of quantity, texture and smell? (quality, ingredients, not digesting properly)
- Does he suffer from flatulence? (quality, ingredients, not digesting properly)
- Does he drink a lot of water? (possibly too salty)
- Does he have any unusual eating habits like eating his own poo / paper tissues / toilet rolls / grass / twigs? (food missing
   something, not being digested properly or a behaviour problem)
- Does he scratch / rub / chew a lot? The usual areas are behind the ears, abdomen/ root of tail / feet /legs. (allergies, ingredients, quality)
- Does he suffer from restlessness or lack of attention? (additives, quality)
-

Any one of the above on its own may not mean a dietary problem, but if there are several perhaps it is time to review your dog's food especially if there are also behavioural problems.

Consult a professional trainer / behaviourist for expert help.

Here are some good indicators when choosing a dry/moist food:-

A named meat source is a good start (chicken, beef), grains such as maize, oats and barley are usually fine but be careful of wheat.

The quality of the ingredients, a good balance of ingredients, digestibility and being free from additives is essential.

In terms of nutrition, **Puppy** food can be up to 29% Protein and then a good follow on **Maintenance** diet would be around 21 – 23% Protein, **Senior** diets for less active older dogs are around 19% Protein.

The pulling dog
Fido Fact – Dogs pull

It is probably the most common problem owners and therefore trainers have to deal with. A walk during which you spend most of the time with your dog at the very end of the lead wishing to get even further ahead is not enjoyable; in fact it can even be dangerous due to the potential loss of control.

So why do dogs pull when on the lead?

Dogs pull for a variety of reasons including:-

- Because they have been allowed to since being a puppy and now assume that this is how you go for a walk
- It is my position / role in the family pack to be in the lead (**Alpha**)
- It is fun to pull and rewarding too. Yes some dogs actually enjoy pulling.
-

Before we start trying to stop the dog from pulling we must check his 'position' in the family /pack to make sure that he knows his place.
 (**See Section 1 - 10 Brave New World**).

We **MUST** ensure that we are **ALPHA**.

Next, it is important to understand three points:-

- a dog does not actually **PULL** they **PUSH** against their collar and that pulls us along.
- a dog can only push against something if there is something to push against – remove the restraint and the dog cannot push.
- If we try to correct a dog's position by pulling back on the lead the dog will resist you. It is called 'negative thigmotaxis'. Grab someone by the sleeve and tug them, they will usually resist!
-

Having checked your dog's position in the household and demoted him as appropriate, two useful pieces of equipment to help in stopping a dog pulling are the **Stop Pull Harness by Walk Your Dog with Love** and the **Happy Chappy** lead.

The **Walk Your Dog with Love** harness is a simple, light weight harness designed to take away choking, pulling, and allow you to lead your dog instead of the usual way round. Most harnesses and collars actually stimulate the dogs desire to pull (push).

Figure of 8 lead (Happy Chappy) (see section 3 equipment).
This lead gives the dog no pain and removes the point of optimum pull from around
the neck to behind the ear on the handler's side and also releases endorphins to
relax the dog making him calmer.

With the either the **WYDWL harness or Happy Chappy** lead fitted properly, and
with a pocket full of treats begin your walk with the dog sitting beside you.
For some dogs even that is asking too much; they get so excited that they start
pulling and rushing around as soon as the lead comes out.

If this is the case start by getting calmness when the lead is put on (**See section 6
lesson calm down it is only a walk**).

Once he can sit quietly at your side with his lead on you can begin the heelwork.

It may be useful for a while to take him by car to a quiet place away from traffic to
start the lesson.
With either device fitted and treats available put your dog to sit holding the loop of
your lead at your waist and say something like '**Let's go'** or '**Off we go'** and begin
your walk. When your dog rushes forward to pull, you stop walking.

DO NOT PULL ON THE LEAD or try to bring him back to the heel position. I
usually say something like '**Oh dear'** or '**Oops'**. It is simply a noise which he will
soon learn means that he has gone wrong.

When you stop moving and say your chosen word/phrase, he will be confused and
will try a range of things to get you walking again.
He may stand still, sit, lay down, faff about, but if you are patient and say nothing
else nor try and help him back into the heel position, just watch him.

Eventually he will come back close enough for the lead to be loose, as soon as this
happens, quickly praise and move off saying '**Let's go'**.

Again as soon as the lead goes tight you stop and the sequence begins again.

 Your dog will begin to see that if he wants to keep going he has to keep the lead
loose.
For some reason a tight lead stops his owner's legs from moving.

Once he has grasped the concept and regularly walks on a loose lead you can
improve his position in the following three ways.
You can use them at different places, where suitable, on your walk which starts
making you more interesting, less predictable and become someone he has to keep
his eye on.

To improve the heelwork position further use the '**Red light / Green light'** exercise (**Section 6 Lessons**)

Once he has grasped the concept and regularly walks on a loose lead you can improve his position in the following three ways.
You can use them at different places, where suitable, on your walk which starts making you more interesting, less predictable and become someone he has to keep his eye on.

- **Remember Me? -** to develop the heel work position you can use the '**do not pull me'** method and just have your lead shorter so it becomes tight as soon as he moves forward in advance of where he should be.
- **Change direction** – holding the lead by the loop every time he goes in front of the heel position turn and go in the
  opposite direction.
  When he catches up and holds the heel position praise resume your original path. This exercise can also be done using the long lead if the area is safe and open enough.
- **Walk back** – When he moves forward to far suddenly walk back 3 or 4 steps, again when he catches up with you resume forward motion and praise when he is beside you.

The Barking Dog

Fido Fact :- Dogs bark!

You do not want to stop your dog barking, just control when it barks. To do this we must understand why dogs bark, once you have identified the why then you can begin the training.

The dog barks excessively for any of the following reasons, in some cases there can be more than one reason.

- **Breed characteristics**
  Some breeds like terriers and hounds have a predisposition to be vocal.

- **Playfulness and excitement**
  This starts as a puppy as a way to encourage someone to play with it. This can develop into barking in anticipation of anything it sees as being exciting.

- **Dominance – see Section 1 Brave New World**
  Staking out its territory.
  Expressing its needs i.e., feed me now or let me out
     Displaying high status in the pack

- **Bad training**
  The owner has inadvertently rewarded barking
     Boredom, insufficient stimulus to mind and body
     Loneliness, insecurity, stressed or uncomfortable
     Improper socialisation
     Attention seeking

- **Danger**
  As a member of a pack it is ok to warn the leader of a potential danger, perhaps a strange person or sound, the dog should stop barking when the leader / alpha shows up.

Fido Fact - Dogs have a better sense of smell, hearing and sight than humans. So just because you can't hear, see or smell anything doesn't mean there is nothing there, your dog knows better.

How to stop excessive barking.

First identify why your dog barks a lot and then make the necessary adjustments as listed below, before you start retraining your dog.

Dominance driven barking- look at how the dog views it's place in the pack (your family) and adjust to lower it's status.

External trigger- perhaps a sound like a phone ringing or a door bell, a person who calls at the house or traffic. In some cases distraction can help.

In some types of barking, especially if the problem is not well established this method can work well.

If you know what sets your dog to bark then just before it happens distract the dog with a simple obedience command like **SIT**. Or a loud clap or whistle which causes the dog to look away from the trigger and focus on you, then reward the dog.

Desensitisation to the trigger can also prove very effective.

Desensitise the dog

This is very effective with sound related barking like the phone ringing or the door bell.
Get someone to phone you or ring the door bell and your dog starts barking, turn your back on the dog and ignore it and of course do not answer the phone or door bell.

Eventually the dog will get confused and receiving no reward from you will stop barking, when it does wait a moment and if it is still quiet praise the dog.
Keep repeating this several times a day for several days, after three weeks repetition with no barking from the dog the lesson is learned.

Often it is responding to your dog when he barked that has taught the dog that if he **'shouts (barks)'** then you reward him by paying attention to him, in which case if you acknowledge him in any way even to scold him he has got his reward.
Instead turn your back on him and pretend he isn't there.

Initially he will try harder, but if you carry on ignoring him he will stop.

When he does stop turn to face him and praise him.

Repeat this lesson every time he barks for attention, and make sure to praise when he lies quietly beside you.

The barking dog
Sometimes you get a dog that just likes being vocal, rather like your chatty aunt, some breeds of dogs also have a predisposition to bark. Therefore why not try teaching the dog to be quiet

In this case having checked that none of the causes for being vocal are contributing then there is only one course of action, to tell your dog what you might like to tell chatty aunty **"BE QUIET!"**

A very effective way to re-educate a dog away from barking is to teach the dog to bark on command. Use the trigger that starts the dog barking and give the command speak and repeat this while the dog barks, praising the dog. No, I have not gone mad!

After a few repetitions of this you give the command just before the trigger and when the dog barks again praise it.
Now it's time to introduce a new command, quiet. After the dog has barked and it stops to draw breath or because the trigger has gone away or stopped give the new command and praise the dog.

Eventually the dog will understand that it must bark when you say speak and cease when you say quiet.
If you never give the command to speak the dog will not bark.

This reprimand must be done carefully, calmly and in a manner that the dog will understand. A powerful tool in the trainers box is the NO command, but this must only be done under the advice and guidance of the trainer.

Training error- Acknowledge where you went wrong and follow the retraining lessons.

Fido Fact – Your dog does not have a problem with its barking. It is you, your family and neighbours that have the problem!

NEVER reward your dog for barking, and **NEVER** commit the three dog training sins, when your dog barks **DO NOT**:-

1) Yell or scream at the dog- it gives attention which acts as a
reward also the dog will think you are joining in and get more excited.

2) Let your dog in or out, feed it or play with it – again this rewards the dog for barking by doing what it told you to.

3) Cuddle, talk soothingly or give treats – this tells the dog you are happy with him and what he is doing.

Time for action
• Asses if dominance is a contributing factor and adjust home life.
• Remove whatever acts as a stimulant
• Avoid leaving dog alone for long periods if this causes barking. Then begin a programme of desensitisation.
• Give plenty of exercise both physical and mental, a tired dog is less likely to bark.

These methods are very effective for controlling barking, but this is not an easy problem to solve and the longer the dog has been barking the longer it will take to control it.

The Chasing Dog

Fido fact – dogs chase

It is part of a dog's survival instinct to chase, otherwise how do you get dinner? In some breeds the instinct is stronger than in others, greyhounds for example.

When our dog chases its first bird in the garden and puts it to flight, we see it as funny, cute and certainly not a dangerous problem.
However this is just the first step to a potentially fatal end.

The domesticated dog chases things for fun and to fulfil a natural instinct, but having had a reward –the bird flying away – he wants to do it again and with each occasion he derives more pleasure.
Soon it is not just birds in the garden, it could be cats, sheep in fact anything that flies or runs away.

 The danger comes from chasing when perhaps chasing a cat, the cat runs across a road and your dog follows and is hit by a car or the car swerves and hits a child.

With sheep and livestock chasing, a farmer can either shoot the dog or if caught demand that it is put down - **Always keep your dog on a lead when around any livestock**.
By teaching your dog a different response to things that fly or run away, perhaps a sit or return to your side you are providing a choice reward for not chasing.

With all dogs that chase, start by providing the opportunity to chase, but make it a ball rather than anything else and make it at your
command. If the dog has not been taught to retrieve things then teach that lesson first – (**See Section 6 - 41 The Retrieve**)

Once the dog understands the exercise and will do it away from birds and animals you can now introduce it where there are birds, perhaps a park or where there is livestock in a field which are not near enough to be troubled and also with the farmer's permission.

Keep the dog on the lead - a long lead is very useful for this exercise as you keep control.

Begin far away from the distraction, roll the ball and give the command to fetch the ball.

Praise and reward for doing it correctly.

If the dog is more interested in the birds then move further away and make the ball more interesting by playing with it yourself and include him when he joins you.

Over time you can gradually move closer to the birds etc.

But do so slowly and only when at that distance the ball is more interesting / fun than the birds.

Livestock

When out walking and you see sheep in a field go by the gate and when the dog sees the sheep give the **'Leave'** command (**See Section 5 -16 Leave it**) and distract with the ball, again making the ball more interesting than the sheep.

When the chasing involves livestock it is worth consulting a professional trainer who has access to some sheep who will not run away, but rather stand their ground or even advance on the dog.
The dog will soon learn to be wary of sheep and not chase.

Never put your dog in with a sheep **'to learn his lesson'** as has been done in the past as that is barbaric and dangerous to all concerned.

The Digging Dog

Fido fact – most dogs will want to dig

Dogs dig, it is a fact of life and they do so for many reasons. In the wild it has a practical purpose like digging to escape danger, making a cooling hollow or warming pit, burying a bone / digging it up later, or searching for food in hard times like roots, bulbs etc.

Some dogs also dig for fun, which is fine unless it is in your bed of prize roses and some dig because they are bored with their lonely life.
Whatever the reason the solution is fairly simple for the domesticated dog.

Firstly establish why given that none of the reasons applicable to the wild dog are applicable to our pet dog – except perhaps to escape, in which case boredom is the problem.

Dogs are very social creatures and even the lowest member of the pack still feels part of that pack.

We take a pup into our homes often without full consideration of what that particular dog's characteristics are and what it will need – perhaps we just like the **LOOK** of that dog / breed?

Sometimes people acquire their pup and expect it to stop behaving like a dog.

They live in immaculate homes, live busy lives and a puddling, chewing, mucky puppy/ dog does not really fit in, but it **LOOKS GOOD** with the image they wish to portray.

In one way or another unwanted behaviour due to poor training, insufficient or inappropriate exercise or just because it is a dog , a dog confined to a small area, often a section of garden with an outside kennel.
For the dog this is hell, he feels abandoned by his pack, bored with nothing to do and he seeks a way to escape or cope with his boredom – he digs.

In these circumstances the owners need to:-
- either change the way they keep the dog by seeking help to redress any training issues and / or provide stimulus and appropriate exercise plus bring the dog into the pack and make him content or
- re-home the dog

Some dogs dig for fun, they are happy, well adjusted dogs who live full and rich lives as part of a family / pack, but they still like to dig. In this case rather than depriving the dog of his pleasure or fighting over it, why not give him his own place to dig?

It is very easy to create a sand pit in a suitable place in the garden, just as you would for a child.
Stock the pit with a few choice and suitable toys slightly buried. This is new to the dog so you will need to show him what to do.

Take him to the pit and encourage him to dig close by a toy then when he finds it praise him.
Move on to another and when found encourage and praise. Repeat a few more times then leave it.
As with all new lessons go back for a few times a day and repeat the exercise.

When you approach the digging pit give a command - perhaps '**digging pit'** - and praise when he gets there. Then encourage him to find and praise when he does.

It will not be long before he will happily use his pit provided you keep it stocked with toys. Then when he goes to dig somewhere he should not, say '**NO – Digging pit'** and take him to his pit and encourage him to dig there with the usual praise. He will soon see that it is **OK** to dig here and not elsewhere.

The Nervous Dog

If any unwanted behaviour will get our sympathy it is a nervous dog. The 'tail up bum, low body carriage, cowering and shaking are all obvious messages recognised by even the most novice handler.

Unfortunately the behaviour is often dealt with in a manner that will encourage the behaviour to continue rather that solving the problem and making the dog feel better.

How many of us would be as sympathetic towards an aggressive dog and yet often these two behaviours are just different manifestations of the same problem.
When dogs get frightened they respond in one of four ways (called the 4 Fs) they will do one of the following:-

FIGHT – FLEE – FREEZE - FAFF

The first two are obvious, the third is that total state of fear that leaves you unsure what to do and so you do nothing.
The last 'FAFF' is that flappy, irrational moving about until you decide what to do or by playing the fool until danger goes away.

The breed characteristics will mean that some dogs have a natural tendency towards one of these reactions and therefore an aggressive dog snarling and barking may be just as nervous as our quivering wreck, but their response is a product of generations of breeding.

Nervousness can also be genetic, so knowledge of the dog's parents, and if possible, grandparents can help.

Feed can also contribute to a dog's nervousness, so seeking the help of a professional can help. There are some dogs, just as there are some humans that are the nervy type.
If you have such a dog and you have noisy, rambunctious children and live a 'full on' life, then a nervous dog will not cope with the lifestyle and re-homing may be the only solution.
Let us assume your dog is generally speaking not the nervy, highly strung type neither were his parents and that your house / lifestyle is not suitable.

Perhaps your dog / pup is meeting new things and is nervous of them, how you handle him will affect whether his nervousness reduces or increases.

When a dog shows fear or apprehension at something we respond (incorrectly) as we would with a nervous child by giving verbal
reassurance, but remember your dog ….

CANNOT UNDERSTAND ENGLISH

"There there Fido, do not worry the nasty thing will not hurt you"

What your dog (FIDO) 'hears is
"Well done FIDO, that's just how I want you to react to the nasty thing because I'm frightened too"

To Fido his behaviour has been rewarded and that this is how we want him to feel and respond. We make things worse than ever by patting, hugging, or if Fido is small enough picking him up and cuddling – double the reward.

If the scary whatever is a person, or a person with a dog, there could be a further reward for Fido when upon seeing that Fido is nervous they stop what they are doing or even move away.

Poor Fido has just learnt that my owners (pack leader) want me to be scared and of course this will get worse until one day Fido can no longer go outside because it is just too scary!

What then should we do to help our apprehensive or nervous dog?

Firstly in consultation with a professional, consider his food to see if this could be the problem, after all, like humans, dogs are what they eat.
(**See section 7– 3 on Food**)

When you meet new things and the dog appears apprehensive, you must remember **YOU** are Alpha and he will be looking to you for guidance.

Therefore 'ced**Be cool'**, show no interest in the scary thing, say nothing at all. Often the distance from something will help, think about your own personal space.
 Allow Fido a bit more room, a long lead enables you to keep control, but allow Fido to create some space without you moving away, which would only confirm his fears.

Regularly seeing the scary thing at a '**safe**' distance will allow your dog to get used to it, to see it is not dangerous and there is no need to be scared. Gradually he will move closer and conquer his fear.

Remember only reward by praising the behaviour you want i.e. if Fido ignores something while remaining relaxed.

In severe cases herbal remedies like one of the **Ayurvedic Animal** range can prove very useful having sought professional help to choose the right product.

These products help to calm the nervous dog while he learns to cope with life's scary things.

It is also believed that increasing the dog's intake of Omega essential fatty acids can help too.

The Protective Dog

If, for whatever reason, your dog has learnt to be protective of 'his' things, he now needs to learn not to guard his things.

Firstly ensure you are enforcing all of the rules of leadership to demonstrate to your dog that you are **ALPHA**.

See (**Section 1-10 Brave New World**)

Sit on a chair, where you can reach the measured amount of food, holding his bowl then follow these guidelines:-

Place some of his food in the bowl and give the dog the command to eat, perhaps '**There you go'**.

After a short while, when the food is gone, drop some more into the bowl and repeat the command to eat.

Each time he empties the bowl drop in some more and then give the command until the meal is eaten.

Do this at each meal and he will soon start to see that being near his food is good and not a threat.

You can gradually introduce a word command to stop eating just as he finishes each portion.

The association will build between the command (perhaps '**Stop'** but said in a regular voice) and his stopping, albeit because there is no food left.

Either way when he lifts his nose out of the bowl, praise and drop in the next portion and give the eat command.

 Gradually build up his confidence by stroking him when he lifts his nose out of the bowl or while he is eating. Place the bowl on the floor and continue the exercise, remove the chair and continue the exercise, but walk around returning to put the next portion in.

He will soon see that rather than being a threat you are there to provide more – how nice.

Once he is happy with you doing this, other family members can repeat the exercise and with each person he will relax quicker.

With toys and chews the approach will need to be different if feeding is also a problem.

Tackle the protection of food first as he will then view your proximity to valued things more positively.

Choose a new toy that he has not had time to see as his '**property**' and remove all others. Allow a few minutes to play then offer him a really tasty treat in exchange for the toy. If he will not give up the toy he does not get the treat, but make sure that it is a really great, smelly treat like a small piece of cooked chicken or beef.

Try this lesson before meals when he will be hungry and the treat becomes more appealing.

Be patient and he will eventually opt for the treat; when he does praise him and then return the toy repeating the exercise two more times. As a lesson repeat this for five times a day. Again he will quickly see that you are not a threat, you can then gradually reintroduce other toys and chews getting other people doing the same.

You can gradually build up his confidence by stroking him when he lifts his nose out of the bowl or while he is eating.
Place the bowl on the floor and continue the exercise, remove the chair and continue the exercise, but walk around returning to put the next portion in.

He will soon see that rather than being a threat you are there to provide more – how nice.

Once he is happy with you doing this, other family members can repeat the exercise and with each person he will relax quicker.

With toys and chews the approach will need to be different if feeding is also a problem.
Tackle the protection of food first as he will then view your proximity to valued things more positively.

Choose a new toy that he has not had time to see as his 'property' and remove all others.
Give him the toy along with the '**Play**' command – See (**Section 2 - 11**)

Allow a few minutes to play then offer him a really tasty treat in exchange for the toy.
 If he will not give up the toy he does not get the treat, but make sure that it is a really great, smelly treat like a small piece of cooked chicken or beef.

Try this lesson before meals when he will be hungry and the treat becomes more appealing.
Be patient and he will eventually opt for the treat; when he does praise him and then return the toy repeating the exercise two more times.

As a lesson repeat this for five times a day.

Again he will quickly see that you are not a threat, you can then gradually reintroduce other toys and chews getting other people doing the same.

The Aggressive Dog

There are many reasons for a dog to be aggressive which can include health problems so if a normally happy dog suddenly becomes aggressive you should consult the vet to see if the dog is in pain thus causing the aggression.

Assuming that there is nothing wrong health wise, we need to study the dog's behaviour.

Consider:-
- When did the aggression start?
- Is another dog / human involved?
- What was happening just before the aggression began?
- How did the dog display aggression?
- What was the dog's body language telling you?

A dog can become aggressive because it feels that it is the only   response available to it. When any dog of any age or breed meets a situation that is unfamiliar or frightening, they have four response options:-

FLIGHT - FREEZE - FAFF - FIGHT

Which option is chosen will depend upon the circumstances like how much socialising they had as a puppy, their training, their breed type, their age and finally the perceived threat.

Aggression includes a range of responses including:-

> Grumbling - growling - snarling - teeth baring - snapping at the air - and bites of varying strengths from barely touching the surface to those which cause serious damage and could result in the dog having to be destroyed.

Certain breed types like terriers and guarding breeds like the German Shepherd and Rottweiler are more prone to use **FIGHT** than say a Labrador or Spaniel which will use **FLIGHT** or **FAFF**.

It is not written in tablets of stone how a breed will respond, much depends on their training and socialisation as this will reduce the likelihood of unwanted behaviour occurring.

Unless something has happened medically, aggression does not suddenly happen; good old Fido does not just wake up today and decide *'I shall bite someone'*.

Dogs and creatures in general, tend to want to avoid a full fight as any injury could prove fatal and as a minimum will impact on survival ability.

Body language is therefore used to communicate a range of signals to express a creature's desire to defuse the situation.

Unfortunately, as a species, human beings are very poor at picking up on human body language, let alone that of a dog.

Your dog has doubtless been sending signals which have gone unnoticed and so in desperation the dog "*suddenly, out of the blue, turned nasty*".
NO, he has been telling you that he is not happy for a while, but you were not 'listening'.

These '**calming signals**' (see **Communicating with your dog**) are   designed to convey the message "I do not want to fight, calm down and let us try and sort this out peacefully."

If the message goes unheeded the dog has no choice other than to communicate more '**clearly**', as we humans would by talking louder / shouting.

To communicate more clearly the dog might:-

*   Bare his teeth
*   Narrow the eyes,
*   Raise his hackles (the hair on the back of the neck)
*   Growl, snarl, even bark or snap.

Reading the body language of certain breeds is hampered by the way they look due to our desire to have '**breed standards**', i.e. docked tails, excessive facial hair, short snouts and heavy set fronts all of which tend to obscure or change the effectiveness of the signals.

How you respond to your '**aggressive**' dog is very important. At the moment he is being aggressive **DO NOT** shout, hit or make any sudden movement, just slightly angle your body away from the dog, do not look directly at the dog and try to look calm.
To your dog loud noises, sudden movements and direct eye contact are all signals of aggression and could trigger the dog to escalate his behaviour.

Stay still, if this eases the situation think about what was happening just before the incident.

Then seek help from a reputable trainer / behaviourist .
It is impossible to outline all the alternative ways to deal with this problem in a book of this nature as everyone's situation is different, but seeking professional help quickly is your best course of action.

Separation Anxiety

Separation anxiety is defined as your dog being greatly distressed whenever you leave, every time you leave.

Scratching at the door, chewing things up, housetraining mistakes, barking hysterically and generally being extremely upset are a few of the sighs.
Most dogs want to be with their humans as much as possible.

Dogs that have not been taught how to stay alone calmly may exhibit unwanted behaviours. Gradually adjusting dogs to being alone is the best approach.
Most puppies and some dogs experience a level of anxiety when left alone, even for very short periods of time.

 Most puppies learn that they are left alone, nothing really bad happens to them, they are still alive, and their '**people**' come back.
They learn how to entertain themselves while alone and gain confidence in their ability to be alone.
As they grow up and gain confidence in themselves, their 'people' can leave them for longer periods of time.

Some dogs, for various reasons, do not gain confidence in themselves. Some dogs are left alone too long when they are puppies and they become traumatised by the event.

Other dogs are neglected or abused and therefore have a low self-esteem.

These dogs can be bounced around from owner to owner and usually end up in an animal shelter.
After they are adopted by well-meaning people they can still carry their low self-esteem and exhibit their learned behaviour of separation anxiety.

Other dogs for unknown reasons have a low tolerance for anxiety.

And lastly, any dog can become traumatised unbeknownst to their '**people**' by some event and can spontaneously begin to experience separation anxiety.

All of these types of dogs can show profound anxiety when being left alone, or simply out of eye-sight of their '**people**'.

The process of teaching them self-confidence and the ability to entertain themselves can be time consuming and requires a lot of patience and positive reinforcement.
Here is how to do it:

Preventing separation anxiety – it is good for your dog or puppy to be comfortable when home alone. You can help him learn this if you take a little time and use these simple steps.

Begin by changing your '**leaving**' routine. Dogs that exhibit separation anxiety usually begin to get anxious long before you walk out the door.

Most people have a set '**leaving**' routine that they go through before leaving the house.

They put their shoes on, close the windows, lock the door, jingle the car keys etc.

Dogs learn this routine very quickly and if they already get anxious from being left alone, this long, drawn out '**leaving**' routine can make matters worse.

When you leave the house, do so promptly. When you leave, say '**Take care of the house'**.

Do not make a big deal out of leaving, just start to teach them a phrase that means ' **I'll be gone, but I'll be back'**. Then when you leave, turn around and come back in after about 30 seconds to 1 minute.

Say hello to your dog in a low-key manner and go about your day. You need to be low-key so that you teach your dog to be low-key.

If you are overly anxious about leaving or coming home you will be conditioning your dog to be anxious as well. The first day, you will leave and come back about a dozen times.

Each time you leave, increase the time you are gone :-

1 minute, 2 minutes, 3 minutes, 5 minutes, 7 minutes, 10 minutes, 15, 20, 30, 45 minutes etc.

Any time you come home and your dog was exhibiting his anxious behaviour (chewing, barking, etc.) cut the time you leave in half next time.

If he is still experiencing separation anxiety, cut your time in half again!; once your dog is no longer anxious, start increasing the times again.

Because of the time and commitment involved in these exercises, it is best if you do this on your vacation for the first week or until you build up to about 4 hours being gone with no anxiety from your dog.

If vacation time is impossible, then start on Friday afternoon or evening, and make this your primary activity for the whole weekend.

Repeat this again the following weekend, varying the time you are gone. Leave for 30 minutes, then for 5 minutes, then for 10 minutes, then for 2 hours, etc.

Dogs are social animals and any dog that spends 8 – 10 hours a day all alone may begin to exhibit obsessive behaviours that may or may not develop into separation anxiety.

A dog that experiences separation anxiety usually does his damage as soon as (or very shortly after) you leave the house.

A dog that is bored and lonely will become destructive after a few hours (usually 4-6) of being left alone.

Another great confidence builder for any dog is training classes.
Even if your dog knows all the obedience commands, he will benefit from a class situation.
Taking your dog to classes increases his confidence in being able to handle new situations.
It also increases his confidence in you as '**leader**'.

Most importantly, it gives him the opportunity to socialise with other dogs and people, and spend quality time with you.

If your dog is an '**only**' dog it is possible that this exacerbates his separation anxiety.

Some dogs that do not have canine companionship become overly dependent on their humans.

Sometimes referred to as '**Velcro-dogs'** (a dog that sticks to you where ever you go), they experience a great amount of stress whenever they are not accompanied by a human.

Although not recommended as a cure-all, you may want to consider getting another dog or puppy for companionship. Another wonderful option is to find a playmate for your dog.

A weekly visit to or from a doggie-playmate's house can be very beneficial to '**only**' dogs (even those that do not suffer from separation anxiety).

Most dogs benefit greatly from canine companionship.

Schedule a playtime for your dog, with another dog that he likes, once or twice a week.

Be sure to spend quality time with your dog.

One-on-one time spent with your dog for 5 -20 minutes a day can help him feel more secure in his environment as well as help strengthen the bond between you both.

Even if you have a Velcro dog, one-on-one time where your attention is focused on your dog is essential.

This quality time should not consist of babying, stroking or cuddling.

Instead, it should consist of doing things to build a strong master / dog relationship and bolster his confidence.

Fun obedience work using positive reinforcement, interspersed with fun games of fetch, chase and hide & seek can be very beneficial for his psychological well-being.

Using a crate

A crate is another good way to prevent or cure separation anxiety
- Start by introducing your dog to his crate
- Crate him for short periods while you are present. Gradually increase the time crated. Reward quiet behaviour with calm praise and perhaps a treat such as a piece of dog food (a healthier option that most treats)
- Start leaving your puppy alone – start with just a few minutes at a time, if possible.
- Gradually increase the time spent alone
- Limit your attention when you are at home so it is not such a shock when you leave.
- Reward your dog with a piece of food and attention when he lies quietly away from you.
-

Most dogs do not need to be crated forever, but do not rush freedom; most dogs are not ready to be given unsupervised freedom in your home until they are 18 months old or older.

For those of you, who work, consider hiring a walker or neighbour to give your dog a midday break. Keeping your schedule similar on weekends as on workdays can help make things easier for your dog.

Exercise – and plenty of it – helps dogs who must be alone long hours.

Do's & don't

Do make leaving and arriving uneventful.

If you make a big production- lots of hugs and goodbyes or asking if he'll miss you – your dog will assume it's a big deal.

When you return do not go directly to his crate or room and make a fuss except if your dog is a young puppy or has been left for many hours.

A note from Keith Fallon

I hope that this book has helped you to understand a little more about your own "Fido" and how she/he ticks.

Whatever your goal may be, competition standard dog or family pet, a dog should be a pleasure to own for many years to come.

The need for good training has never been greater with more responsibility on dog owners to have a well behaved dog.

Modern dogs have more pressure than ever, fulfilling a multitude of roles companion, guard dog, worker, fashion accessory.

At the end of the day the modern dog is still a dog, fairly simple and straight forward.

Understanding your dog, training, exercise, good strong boundaries (he knows where he should fit in) and an appropriate diet are key to a happy dog.

Thanks to **Nadine Carr** for the hours we spent practising gun dog training using the methods in this book with her spaniel Bramble.

Also to the countless dogs and owners that I have had the privilege of knowing and training.

Finally to my own dogs Skye & Pipin, two cheeky spaniels that never fail to raise a smile for their endless enthusiasm and happy go lucky nature.

Keith Fallon - *Cheltenham, April 2016*

Master Dog Trainer, Behaviourist, Director Cotswold Pet Services Ltd

25035224R00092

Printed in Great Britain
by Amazon